KNOW

YOU ARE

BELOVED

KNOW YOU ARE BELOVED

Press Pause, Breathe Deeply,
and Be Known by God

———— ✦ ————

REV. CHRIS LEE

TYNDALE
MOMENTUM®

A Tyndale nonfiction imprint

Visit Tyndale online at tyndale.com.

Visit the author online at revchris.org.

Published in association with The Bindery Agency, www.TheBinderyAgency.com.

For information about special discounts for bulk purchases, please contact Tyndale House Publishers at csresponse@tyndale.com, or call 1-800-323-9400.

Library of Congress Cataloging-in-Publication Data

A catalog record for this book is available from the Library of Congress.

ISBN 978-1-4964-7464-3

Printed in China

30	29	28	27	26	25	24
7	6	5	4	3	2	1

For the reader, know you are loved!

CONTENTS

———————— ✟ ————————

AN INVITATION TO BREATHE

This is what the LORD says: "Stand at the crossroads and look;
ask for the ancient paths, ask where the good way is,
and walk in it, and you will find rest for your souls."

JEREMIAH 6:16

We live in a unique time.

Our days are filled with images, text, and noise, continually streaming from a screen that all of us obsessively carry. It weighs us down. Its beeps clamor for our attention, and all of this distraction is wearing us thin.

We have been through—and are going through—a great unsettling in our world. What once satisfied simply doesn't anymore. We are united in a sense of our fragility and mortality. As the biblical poet once put it, "We are dust" (Psalm 103:14).

We have been shaken.

This has left us startled and dazed.

There was a guy who started his faith journey at a young age, growing up in a Christian family. He was involved with Christian outreach and ministries to the needy. Eventually he started working in a busy industry of information and technology, and he did very well. But with his success came more demands. He threw himself into it and worked very hard, but his relationships started to suffer as the demands on his time grew. When he did spend time with his family or friends, he would repeatedly check his phone. He had constant access to the world, and the world and his job had constant access to him. He was not bad, just busy. He started to become less present, his depth of character suffered—and his relationship with God suffered. As he became more in the eyes of the world, he became less within himself. Where once there was a guy who laughed a lot and loved those around him, in his place was a more fragile, more distracted, harder person. Not mean, but just colder; not bad, but less compassionate and engaged. In a sense he had good soil, as Jesus talks about in Matthew 13, but no longer deep soil. This guy embodies a whole generation. I see many like him— even I am like him at times. Perhaps you recognize yourself in him too. We all have such a wonderful capacity for depth and beauty, yet we swim in the shallows distracted by many things. Our screen time is up, and our prayer time is down.

In this cultural moment where we are so highly connected and available all the time, I meet a lot of men and women who are asking questions of identity: "Who are we? What's our place in all of this? Why are we here?" These are questions that touch on eternity, and they will only be answered by eternity.

The problem is that we live restless lives. There is always something near us—whether it is Netflix or a news feed—that can give us quick stimulation. We rush from place to place, disoriented by the outrage of the moment. We are not built to take on the thousands of concerns thrown at us daily, on top of our own personal struggles. In response, we start to become numb in order to survive it all. We fall victim to dopamine hit after hit, and we wonder why anxiety rises and we feel tired the whole time.

I wrote this book to encourage an escape from this chaos—a place to sit still and breathe, to go deeper with God and ourselves. We need to relearn how to welcome God into this present moment.

The quote at the start of this introduction comes from the book of Jeremiah, where the prophet encourages Israel—troubled and besieged—to look back to the old ways, the good practices, to once again live by God's law in order to find peace. Our senses are under siege today, and we are often losing the battle. I have personally found so much inspiration from great historical church figures such as the Desert Fathers and St. Francis of Assisi in particular. Their teachings are often overlooked, yet they are so relevant to our current experience. Through wars and conflicts, through political unrest and upheaval, these teachers of the church struggled with the same questions we ask today. The truths of God don't change. They were as true then as they are now. When I started leading a church a few years back, I also started sharing these kinds of thoughts on Instagram in sixty-second sermons. People resonated with the spiritual break I was offering on social media. That's when I decided to write a book that would help people to fight back, put down their phones, sit before God, and know their place in Him and their identity as His beloved. In this book, I have written concise chapters that refocus us on simple yet profound truths, borrowing from the lessons of great historical Christian teachers. My goal is to help us rediscover the ancient paths so that we can walk in peace.

At the end of each chapter, I offer a place to *breathe* deeply and sit in silence—an opportunity to focus on what's most important.

My prayer is that this book may help you find moments that calm your spirit and turn your gaze to God.

You *can find* peace, security—more fullness in your life.

You *can know* beyond a shadow of doubt that you are seen—and that God delights in you.

You are His beloved.

Join me on this journey.

PART I

BECOMING

HUMAN

WHO AM I?

Lord, who are you? And who am I?

ST. FRANCIS OF ASSISI

"Teach me who You are. Teach me who I am." What a simple, almost perfect prayer.

It is pregnant with meaning and depth, yet communicates with a classic simplicity that resonates today.

Who are You? Who am I?

The world loves to inform us of who we are. But who does God say we are?

As a vicar, I have the privilege of walking with people as they navigate their lives. One congregant at my church is a student at the Royal College of Music. That school was recently rated first in the world for music, just nipping Juilliard to the title. My friend is an incredible flutist: she won a competition in her college, making her arguably the best flutist in the school. On top of that, she was handed a place to carry on studying after her degree is completed. She is good—really good. I was so happy for her, but as I walked and talked with her, I could sense that she couldn't shake the feeling that she is not good enough. After she won the competition, her immediate thoughts went to *I only won because I fluked it. I got lucky.* She has this refrain playing over her life: *I'm not good enough.* Here is literally the best flutist, in the best college on earth, arguably making her one of the best flute players in the world, and every time she plays, she thinks she is not good enough. Together, we tried to dismantle this lie.

Many of us hear that same voice in our lives.

What is the lie that you believe about yourself? You need to dismantle it and start building on the rock that is Christ and what the Bible teaches us about ourselves, that we are written on the palm of His hands (see Isaiah 49:16), that He knows every hair on our heads (see Matthew 10:30), and that nothing on heaven or earth can separate us from His love (see Romans 8:38-39). I love that St. Francis asks God, "Who am I?" God is the only source of the true answer.

We are each created with the divine stamp deep inside, which whispers to us that our identity as humans comes from God. The first, most important thing about who we are is that we are loved, that our worth doesn't come from the words or actions of others, or our own achievements or lack thereof. Our starting point is that we are loved by God—we are His, *beloved*. We are not like the grit in an oyster that over time, with God's grace, becomes a pearl. We start off profoundly precious. At the beginning of our story, we are created good. We are of infinite worth because we are infinitely loved by an infinite God. This is where we start. I'm not saying we are perfect. We do sin. The Fall happened and is part of our story. We get it wrong. We get hurt, and we hurt. But none of this affects who we truly are or who God created us to be.

This first part of the book is titled "Becoming Human." When using this phrase, I'm acknowledging that we often forget ourselves, lose sight of who we are, and flounder around in the dark seeking anything we can find to teach us about our worth: an Instagram post, a touch from another, words of praise, an action we did or didn't do. The refrain from our heart to the world can be "teach me who I am," and too often we fall victim to bowing before the idols of sex, money, power, and success to learn about ourselves. We think having the most shows we are happy, when really it is the opposite: needing the least illustrates that we are at peace. We need to unlearn some things and learn again to become human. God is the only true source of understanding our identity. Interestingly, the root of the word *understand* comes from an old English word meaning "between" or "among" rather than beneath.[1] It is as we stand among God, stand with God, that we can truly *under*stand ourselves.

There is the knowledge that comes from reading Scripture and acknowledging what it says about humanity and what God has done to show us His love. It is obvious that God loves us, all of us, and since our inception has been bringing us to Himself, in the same way that as a father I want to be loved by my children and I want them to know my love. God literally sent His own Son into the world, who then laid down His life for us. If He was willing to do that, what won't He do for us? As the apostle Paul puts it, "He who did not spare his own Son, but gave him up for us all—how will he not also, along with him, graciously give us all things?" (Romans 8:32).

Sometimes pride can be an issue when we say, "I am not worthy of God's love." That is pride because it actually implies the possibility of earning God's love—that there could be a time when you do enough to deserve it. But it's not about what we do. It's not about making ourselves good enough to be loved. He already loves us. Let us simply acknowledge that God loves us and that this love is not fleeting. It cost Him. It is not passive; it is active, and it is chasing you at every moment of your existence. So stop and let yourself be enfolded by Him. Let yourself receive His love.

Breathe.

Remember:
I was created good.
Who I am is found in God alone.

The way something begins is important, and in the Bible both the Old Testament and New Testament begin with creation. It is interesting to note that every character who has a birth narrative goes on to do something of great importance for God, both in the Old Testament and New Testament. These birth narratives are not given to everyone—just a select few: for example, Adam, Moses, Jacob and Esau, Samson, John the Baptist, and of course Jesus. The birth of things mentioned shows God's involvement and signifies a great plan. Genesis starts with the creation of everything in the universe: God's Spirit hovering over the waters and God speaking His creation into being. Two Gospels—Matthew and Luke—begin with the birth of Jesus. God's Spirit comes upon Mary, and Jesus is conceived, both divine and human. That is the mystery of the Incarnation. I love the way that the start of the Gospel of John brings both together—the story of Creation and the story of the Incarnation, merging both the cosmos and the birth of Jesus. It starts with "in the beginning was the Word" (John 1:1), mirroring the first verse of Genesis, "In the beginning God created the heavens and the earth." Then John continues with "the Word became flesh" (verse 14), which takes us forward to the birth of Jesus. We were created because of a loving God, who has a great purpose for humanity. Jesus was sent by a loving God to a world that He loves. As John 3:16 tells us, "For God so loved the world that he gave his one and only Son, that whoever believes in him shall not perish but have eternal life."

One of the most amazing claims the Bible makes about God is that "God is love" (1 John 4:8). It is not just that God loves, or that to love is good, but that God Himself is love. This is a wonderful and uniquely Christian claim. The apostle John knew all about God's love. He referred to himself often as "the disciple whom Jesus loved" (John 13:23; 21:20), a bold claim. But not perhaps as arrogant as it may first come across. John knew Jesus. He knew His love, and he saw all that Jesus went through that showed His love, so he could boldly say, "Jesus loved me" or perhaps more accurately, "Jesus loves me." You and I can know this love too. We can say, "I am beloved of God." The problem I see is that we can get caught up in the judgment of God and in the accusatory nature of our own sin. We rightly see ourselves as fallen, but when we take our eyes off ourselves and put them back on God, we can see again the great love He has for us in spite of all our weaknesses. As C. S. Lewis wrote,

> If God is Love, He is, by definition, something more than mere kindness. And it appears, from all the records, that though He has often rebuked us and condemned us, He has never regarded us with contempt. He has paid us the intolerable compliment of loving us, in the deepest, most tragic, most inexorable sense.[2]

I have officiated at many weddings in my life as a priest. They are always great occasions. Often the Bible reading selected for the wedding service is the famous chapter 1 Corinthians 13. Let's look at the first few verses:

> If I speak in the tongues of men or of angels, but do not have love, I am only a resounding gong or a clanging cymbal. If I have the gift of prophecy and can fathom all mysteries and all knowledge, and if I have a faith that can move mountains, but do not have love, I am nothing. If I give all I possess to the poor and give over my body to hardship that I may boast, but do not have love, I gain nothing.
>
> I CORINTHIANS 13:1-3

This is one of the best descriptions of love in the Bible. The apostle Paul goes on to describe the attributes of love, but if God is love as John tells us He is, then you could replace *love* here with *God*. Let me show you how it reads if you do that in the next several verses:

> God is patient, God is kind. He does not envy, He does not boast, He is not proud. He does not dishonor others, God is not self-seeking, He is not easily angered, He keeps no record of wrongs. God does not delight in evil but rejoices with the truth. He always protects, always trusts, always hopes, always perseveres. God never fails.
>
> 1 CORINTHIANS 13:4-8

It is powerful stuff! God is love, and you are His beloved.

Another equally amazing claim is that when God created us—you and me—He created us in His "image" (Genesis 1:26). We are created by love and from love and in love. Thomas Merton describes it well: "To say that I am made in the image of God is to say that love is the reason for my existence, for God is love. Love is my true identity. Selflessness is my true self. Love is my true character. Love is my name."[3]

The deepest you is love, and love is the language you were formed by.

You were conceived and made in love.

You are lovely, and you are loved.

Can we all breathe now . . . and start from here?

This is why the gospel is "Good News." When we think about the Christian message—its genesis, its beginning, which is your beginning, it's part of your birth narrative—it is good. It says that you are loved, and you are God's own.

Think about that: the deepest part of you is love. You were formed in love. Too many of us—including me—doubt this deep down. Do you believe this about yourself?

You are loved.

You belong to God.

———————— ✣ ————————

Breathe.

Remember:
The deepest me is love.
I am loved.

2

WELCOME TO THE TABLE

The earth is the LORD's, and everything in it,

the world, and all who live in it.

PSALM 24:1

Because we live in England, tea is important to us. My
wife drinks more tea than anyone else I have ever met.
If someone comes into our home, the first thing to do
is put the kettle on. We have one of those kettles that glows
when it heats up. The sides are transparent, so you can see the
water inside bubbling, and then comes the satisfying click when
it is done. It is funny, the sound of the bubbling water can be
therapeutic, as my body knows I am about to sit with friends
and loved ones and just be. If friends compliment me on a
good cup of tea, I sometimes joke, "It was made with love,"
the best ingredient. In a simple way, sitting and having a cup
of tea with someone is quite a holy thing.

So why is it holy to have a cup of tea? Well, the adjective

holy comes from the Old English word *hālig* and is related to the German word *heilig*, meaning "blessed." There is a relationship between *holy* and being *whole*. *Holy* is synonymous with being *set apart*. There is something whole, something complete about being in a loving relationship, about the giving and receiving nature of loving relationships. Sharing a moment, such as having a cup of tea together, is taking time to be present with someone, creating space, setting other things aside so you can spend time, and forgetting the rest of the world to be with each other, which is holy and loving.

The famous Trinitarian icon *Trinity*, sometimes called the *Hospitality of Abraham*, was painted by Andrei Rublev in the early fifteenth century. It appears to depict three people sitting around a little coffee table having a cup of tea, welcoming you to join them. I find it interesting that this image of three people around the table is probably the best-known depiction of the Trinity. It is based on the story in Genesis 18 where three visitors come to Abraham and Sarah. Abraham encourages them to stay and be refreshed. He offers them food and water, and they sit and eat with him: "Let me get you something to eat," Abraham says, "so you can be refreshed and then go on your way—now that you have come to your servant" (Genesis 18:5).

They answer him, "Very well . . . do as you say" (verse 5).

After receiving his hospitality, the visitors tell Abraham that Sarah will bear a child.

They stay, sit, eat, and drink, and then they bless Abraham and Sarah. The whole interaction is a wonderful picture of the divine joining the human world in a mutual welcome which leads to blessing. This story from Genesis is one of invitation and acceptance. The *Hospitality of Abraham* icon invites us into the meeting. We are invited to sit at the table with God. Who we are is found in who God is, wholeness found in holiness, identity found in being with God. We are loved because God is love.

Sometimes all you need is a friend and a good cup of tea. God wants to spend time with us and enjoys spending time with us—not because He has to out of some duty. He created us. He called us good. He loves us—and, I believe, likes us.

Creation comes out of love. Love is open, humble, and giving. Love is by its very nature a constant offering of itself, the way in which light gives out of itself. It would not be light otherwise. Love is inherently relational; it shares itself by its nature. This is part of the mystery of the Trinity: Father, Son, and Holy Spirit are enfolded in a loving relationship. Our God is relationship—giving out of Himself and welcoming into Himself. It is in prayer that we are welcomed into love, recognizing our image found in the image of the loving Creator. We are, if you like, brought home to ourselves in God. What I mean is that we can often feel like strangers to ourselves and the world around us, but when we find God, we begin to find our true identity and our place in the world. Our worldview shifts from us being the center of the universe and trying to make sense of everything based on our experiences, to seeing ourselves caught up in something much bigger with greater purpose and meaning. People used to think that the earth was the center of the universe and everything revolved around it, until they discovered that the earth revolves around the sun! It is in relationship with God that we discover this new perspective and our true place. It is in prayer that this new life is revealed to us in Jesus and enabled by the breath of love found in the world that is the Holy Spirit.

You are being invited to the table.
Will you sit?
Take some time.
Rest and reflect.

Breathe.

Be known.
Be loved.

3

◈

LISTEN TO THE
WHISPERS OF TRUTH

Are not two sparrows sold for a penny? Yet not one of
them will fall to the ground outside your Father's care. And
even the very hairs of your head are all numbered. So don't
be afraid; you are worth more than many sparrows.

MATTHEW 10:29-31

G
od watches over you. You are never outside of His
care.

You are loved by God and created good—all great
news.

But . . . and this is a big *but*.

Our experience in this world is that we hurt.

Some of the most amazing people I know are also the ones
who have suffered the most. I have a good friend whom I met
at college. He approached me out of the blue during our first
few days there and told me that God had told him to pray with
me. I was startled, yet I believed him. We have been praying
together for the last twenty years. He is full of the Holy Spirit,

21

an amazing, humble guy who has spoken into my life more times than I can count and who continues to inspire me to this day. But he has had a difficult life. His parents died in a plane crash in South America when he was twelve. My friend was told by his headmaster, who asked him to come to his office. My friend thought he was in trouble, only to receive the shocking news that his parents had died. I can't imagine how difficult this would have been. From then on, my friend and his sister were raised by their uncle. My friend struggles with mental health issues and has not had a full night's sleep for as long as I have known him. He goes through great lows, and it is difficult to witness. Many times, I have prayed for this thorn to leave him, to no avail. Yet this man is holy, a wonderful pastor, husband, father, and friend. He reminds me to trust God in the valley as well as on the mountaintop—and that we are not a perfect people, but we do have a perfect God.

But, you may say, how could a loving, all-powerful God allow all this pain? Surely God is either not all-powerful or not all-loving? This question is a fair one and is probably the single greatest reason that people do not believe in God or turn away from Him in their journey of faith. We all suffer, like my friend who lost his parents, or like my wife and me who suffered three miscarriages. How could a good God allow this? I haven't heard a totally satisfying answer to this. People of faith throughout all of history have asked these questions and been left wondering.

None of the answers given are satisfying. For instance, someone might say, "What doesn't kill you makes you stronger." Nope! Think of the abused person who has suffered at the hands of someone over many years. They are not stronger because of this trauma; they are not better off!

What about the argument of free will? The reasoning is that God gives us free will, but we often choose to reject Him, and we are the ones who cause pain. I agree, but also I believe in miracles. I believe God acts. I believe people of faith pray in faith, and sometimes nothing happens but occasionally it does. So if He does change things in certain situations, why not in all? The free will argument falls a little flat when we see God acting in some places and not others. For instance, the apostle Paul was once a persecutor of the church, but Jesus revealed Himself to Paul on the road to Damascus (see Acts 9:1-19). Paul was converted by this experience, and he became the greatest evangelist of the church. Where was the free will there? Would any of us really turn away from God following such a vision? Maybe, but stories like this show that God can and does act when He chooses and is not bound by human free will.

More recently, the idea of "process theology" has emerged, which, as I understand it, tries to argue that God is not all-powerful. According to this view, God cannot control anything, not even a worm; He can only influence. Again this does not fit or satisfy me in any way, as it limits God. My understanding is you cannot find any foolproof answer to the problem of evil—after all, why was the snake in the Garden in the first place? There has to be a place for humility, which chooses to trust God even when we don't understand Him and which does not patronize the sufferings that people go through.

The hard truth is everyone experiences pain, and many of us often feel separated, isolated, and alone. You can tell me that God loves me, but holding on to that love is a challenge. All of us feel unlovable in some way. The question lies with each of us: How will we react to the pain and evil we experience? Are we willing to trust in the knowledge that God loves us rather than depend on how we feel, or will we look to the world for answers and dismiss God? Will we seek—like Job, who lost everything—to stick with God? We may scream and shout and wail at Him, as Job did, but Job never cursed God (see Job 2). In fact, the struggle, the wailing, the annoyance, and the frustration with God in times of pain shows we are walking with Him.

Going back to my friend who has suffered a lot and who is a fantastic priest, he constantly doubts his ability and second-guesses his leadership. All who know him, know him to be a fantastic leader and pastor, but it is easier to hear the bad stuff which shouts in our minds rather than the whisper of truth which tells us we are loved. His answer is lean into God, to lay down his thoughts and insecurities, and to listen again to God in prayer.

———————— ✦ ————————

When we read the beginning of Genesis, we see how God created things and said they were good. God created, and at five different points the passage tells us "God saw that it was good" (Genesis 1:10, 12, 18, 21, 25). Then He created humans, and we are recorded as the seventh good—in fact we are called "very good" as God reviewed all that He had made (verse 31). You may know that numbers have an importance within the biblical narrative, which adds to the meaning of what they describe. Just as I like words and their meaning, I also enjoy learning about numbers and their symbolism. The number seven is linked with creation and used to help describe something's completeness, its fulfilled or finished work on both a physical and spiritual level. The word *created* describes God's creative work seven times in the first couple chapters of Genesis (1:1, 21, 27 (three times); 2:4). In the book of Revelation, we read of seven churches, seven angels, seven seals, seven trumpets, seven thunders, and the seven plagues. The first resurrection of the dead takes place at the seventh trumpet. There are many other examples in the Bible of the significance of this number. You may say, "Oh, come on, you can find patterns in anything if you look hard enough," and you would be right. But many biblical scholars agree that numbers take on special meaning in the Bible, and in this case humanity as the seventh good means we hold a special place in creation. You see, you are of more value than many sparrows!

Rarely does a preacher tell people something new. I usually share a truth that people already know, or I remind them of something they once knew and forgot. We all know that we aren't supposed to find our worth in things like success, wealth, physical attractiveness, and so on. But in the world today, there can be such an onslaught of noise that it's hard to discern what is true. It is like navigating through the fog, trying to find a sense of direction when everything is concealed. That is *very* difficult. The rise of the Internet has given birth to many kinds of social media, which now have almost 5 billion users.[1] With so much ongoing communication, it has become really hard to find any certainty. We hear about digital echo chambers and algorithms directing what comes up in our feeds. There is a vast variety of "unfiltered" posts and worrying misinformation. The barrage of lies masquerading as truth is endless, and we see in the news the victims who get caught up in these untruths.

Being on Instagram as a Christian influencer is a real privilege. I actually use the number seven in my handle, revchris7. I needed a number since revchris was taken, and I chose seven for its biblical meaning. I love speaking about God and helping people discover Him, but I need to be careful too. God is not bothered about success; He wants obedience and a heart turned towards Him. It is easy to disguise pride, arrogance, and insecurity behind a successful profile. The devil is not stupid; he will try to get us to fall any way he can. I have to keep coming back to simple truths, without which I could become conceited and lose touch with reality. I must work at remembering why I am posting and what my purpose is on social media. I keep myself accountable to people I trust and give them permission to ask me questions or challenge me. I also ask myself where I need to be careful, what my weaknesses are, and where I am likely to be tempted. Without these reflections, I can get caught up in campaigns I don't fully understand and political arguments that lead nowhere. I risk gaining an inflated ego or engaging in conversations that may compromise my true calling. I get lots of DMs (direct messages) on Instagram. I read a lot of them, but I won't respond to anyone I don't know directly or who is not acquainted with someone I know. The sad truth is that I read many messages that talk about self-harm and suicide. I also receive a number of messages from bored men and women who try to be flirtatious. Mostly I hear from well-meaning people who want some guidance, but I can't be a local vicar and an individual pastor to thousands of people around the world. I simply do not have the time. I'm here to let people know God exists and loves them, as well as to encourage them to join a loving community in a church near them.

We need to keep coming back again and again to the simple foundational truths of our existence. That is why I have been quoting Scriptures related to our identity and our creation and using them to help show us our true selves. When we do that, we are perhaps more able to hear and believe the whisper of truth by the Holy Spirit, rather than the shout of the world. We are fighting an uphill battle in this loud and aggressive world clamoring for our attention.

————— ✛ —————

Breathe.

Listen to the whisper of truth.

————— ✛ —————

When I was starting my vocation as a priest, I worked for three years in a homeless ministry. I was in charge of the pastoral care of guests who came to our drop-in, where they could rest and get some food and support. I loved this time and probably learnt more here about ministry and leadership than I did anywhere else. But I also learnt a disturbing truth. A shockingly high proportion of those who live on the street believe in conspiracy theories. Mental health issues—or an unhappy, hurt, and sometimes angry outlook on the world—lead many to be susceptible to wild and dangerous beliefs. Some people I met took these ideas as fact. While this is an extreme example of believing lies, it has been worrying to see in our world the many people who are falling victim to off-the-wall conspiracy theories. With the rise of social media, this problem has only been compounded.

In church we often repeat simple truths to keep us rooted in what's important. I'm sure you have heard your pastor repeat himself if you attend church! If you ever come to my church for a significant time, you will recognize a pattern to my sermons. Most are formed around the simple truth that God loves you and is with you through it all. We all face a war of attrition for our souls, and often it seems that the world is winning as it uses everything at its disposal to tell us what it wants. The world says, "You are what you own," as in, "You don't have a nice car or a nice house. You are really poor, and poor means bad, so you are bad." It tells us, "You are what others say you are, so seek their approval, get on their good side, gossip about someone you think they don't like." It tells us, "You are what you do. You are only as good as your successes or your failures—and your failures are far easier to remember, so you will always feel inadequate."

We can, however, overcome this constant barrage. We can break free of these lies. We can know and feel God's love. It is possible to experience the freedom we hear preached.

———————— ✦ ————————

The hard truth is that we need to
practice living out this truth.
Listen to it.
Hold on to it.
Come back to it.
Believe it.
You are loved by God.

Breathe.

I am more than the sum of my feelings.
Hold on to truth.
Believe it.

4

COME AS YOU ARE

Let the little children come to me.

MATTHEW 19:14

On a family trip to the Greek island Kefalonia, I heard a traditional Greek Orthodox story from a friend's father who helped support an Orthodox chapel on a steep mountainside there. According to the legend, there were three fishermen who got caught in a great storm off the coast. Their boat was being thrown around, and they knew that death was imminent. They prayed to God to save them and vowed that in exchange for their survival, they would devote themselves to Him in prayer. The boat broke up, but they managed to be swept to shore on a large piece of wood. Seeking to honor their vow, they gave themselves to prayer. Other fishermen who passed the island shared stories about these miracle men of prayer.

Eventually, a bishop heard about their faith and wanted to visit the men to learn from them. He got to the island and was disappointed to find three uneducated men who knew very little about the faith. Seeking to guide them, he taught them a simple prayer. Then he got back in his boat and left. However, a shout went out from the others in the boat that there were men in the water. The bishop looked over the boat's edge, and there were the three men running towards the boat on the water. When they reached the side of the boat, they asked the bishop to remind them of the words of the prayer, which they had already forgotten. Seeing the men on the water, the bishop was amazed and said, "Carry on with what you have been doing. God is with you."

There's something about this legend that resonates with me. I love the idea that God is accessible to all people who seek Him, not just the most intelligent or the most well read. Come as you are. The faith of an academic is not more valid than the faith of a regular person. They may both know God equally well.

If you went to the gym once and someone asked, "Hey, is it making a difference?" you would say, "Not yet." But after several months of going a few times a week, you might notice the difference and say yes to this question. There is a difference between someone who goes once and expects to see immediate results and someone who is willing to persist over months. We need to persist in the truth to see it affect us. Christianity and its truths are better caught than taught. It is a way of living and being rather than a contract of belief we sign up to. Often we hear things like "Our actions flow from our beliefs." But I would say that the relationship here between what we believe and how we act is more complex than that. We can put God in a box and keep Him at arm's length, pulling Him in from time to time to make ourselves feel good, then pushing Him out again so as to not get too uncomfortable with our way of living. It is our actions which indicate our beliefs. Does our faith in Christ affect how we live? If we were in a court of law, accused of being a Christian, would the evidence of our lives point to this or not? However, this does not mean it's easy to surrender our sinful habits upon becoming a Christian. There are times our faith and actions may contradict each other. Someone may struggle with an addiction they know is wrong and goes against their beliefs, for instance. We are all on a journey of becoming more Christlike, where grace is the rule, not the exception. Don't think that you need to have everything figured out before you approach God. We don't need to have all of our theology sorted out in order to come to Jesus.

The early church didn't have some of the language that we use today to describe God and the Trinity. Those early pioneers in the church did not understand certain things about God and all that He was doing in Christ. Remember, the very early Christians didn't have the Bible as we have it today. It was all written down in varying forms by AD 100 but it wasn't really compiled and put together until about AD 400 by St. Jerome. But they got on, worshiped, prayed, and followed the living God—and more understanding came. Theology is important. But first, if you are seeking God, sit down and pray.

———————— ✛ ————————

Breathe.

Come to Him as you are.

Sit.

Pray.

FOLLOW ME

Then come, follow me.

MATTHEW 19:21

I remember sitting on my bed in my small room at
Cambridge University, the light pouring into the room
from the window overlooking the court, simply transfixed.
Mesmerized. Discovering the Desert Fathers was so powerful
and humbling for me. When I first came to God and started a
relationship with Jesus, it was easy for me to slip into the mind-
set that I knew God now. I had gone from no relationship with
God to a relationship with Him, and that was it. What I failed
to realize was that for two thousand years, people far wiser and
holier than I had been walking with God. There was a lot I
could learn from them. People talk about Christianity being a
relationship and not a religion. But that can be too simplistic
an understanding. The term "religion" is loaded, and people

use it to mean different things. Usually it seems to build a gap between God and man, but the way I use and see the word is that it can actually build a bridge. Let me explain what the practice of religion refers to in my mind: it embodies prayer, spiritual exercises, confession, taking the Eucharist, service, worship—all actions that help to build a relationship with God, not distance us from Him. Sometimes people say they don't like religion—and they have good reasons. Controlling, even abusive churches exist, sadly. But sometimes people say they don't like religion because they really don't like being told what to do. When I first came to Jesus, I thought it was all about me and God. I didn't need anyone else to tell me about God because I knew Him now.

The thing is, there is a lot to know about our faith, and the church and religion can help us discover this through well-tested practices. Our relationship to Jesus is not based on feelings alone. It is deeper. It demands much of us. The Desert Fathers understood this, and they inspired me with their devotion and insight into walking with God. I was hooked and wanted to know more about these people who literally gave up everything in order to live their lives before God. One of the most profound things is that as they pushed into God—as they became closer to Him—they realized the nature of God: His amazing love, His transforming grace. They found their place revealed more truly in Him as beloved children of the living

God. They became immovable in their faith. The place they were found was love. They sat in the very furnace of love and allowed themselves to burn within it.

Before coming to college, I spent some time living in rural Tanzania in East Africa. I quit my job and left everything I knew in search of a deeper, more reliant relationship with God. The part of Tanzania where I lived was very remote, and picking up the *Life of Antony* by Athanasius made so much sense of this time. Anthony the Great was known as the father of monks, as he was one of the first ever monks and certainly the most influential. He left everything he knew and went into the desert in search of God. My time in Africa felt a little like going into the desert as Anthony did centuries ago. Going into the unknown in search of God, I recommend this: you will need courage, but courage is the midwife for calling. My time in Tanzania was incredibly formative. It is hard to know the full extent of the influence it had upon me. I found faith on the lips of everyone I met. I was woken up every morning by sung worship from the beautiful voices of about a hundred people. It was the best alarm clock ever! I made friends for life, and it was a great time of growth and healing for me. I praise God for my time there. I saw things which were darker too. I interacted with witch doctors, had my first experiences of the demonic, and witnessed unusual things that were hard to explain. I felt like I had entered into a cosmic battle and had no reference for it.

The stories I read about St. Anthony—his battling demons, performing miracles, and "turning the desert into a city"[1] were compelling and oddly made sense in light of my experience in Tanzania. His profound piety appealed to me and excited me, and I wanted to find out more. He moved into the desert around AD 286 and did not emerge for many years. As the news of him spread, many people came to him, and he founded many monastic communities. Anthony died in AD 356 at 105 years of age. But his work was carried on by other greats including Abba Pambo, John the Dwarf, Abba Poemen, Basil of Caesarea, Evagrius Ponticus, Arsenius the Great, Moses the Black, Macarius the Great, and women, too, such as Syncletica of Alexandria, Theodora of Alexandria, and Amma Sarah of the Desert. This list of Desert Fathers and Mothers is just scratching the surface. There were of course many, many more.

They all had a lot to say about a great many things, which is ironic as much of their teaching was around remaining silent. We are blessed to have so many of their sayings written down. Sometimes these teachings were called "words." A student would come to a father (an older monk) and say, "Father, give me a word." These lessons were the source of many of the monks' teachings.

To me, the Desert Fathers and Mothers are giants of the Spirit, those who threw off every trapping in life with a single pursuit in mind: loving Jesus Christ. Their love for God is profoundly inspiring. It was an amazing time in history when the Spirit of God called many into the desert—as He called Jesus after His baptism (see Mark 1:12). What came out of that movement is a legacy we still benefit from today. One writer and lover of the desert tradition, Metropolitan Anthony of Sourozh, inspired by their action, said the following of the Desert Fathers: "The King of Love must be enthroned in our mind and heart, take undivided possession of our will, and make of our very bodies the Temples of the Holy Ghost."[2]

I find the all-encompassing commitment from these Christians inspiring. To them, the mind, heart, soul, and body were all for devotion to God. They lived this out not just in words but actions.

You may not have heard of the Desert Fathers, so let me give you some background. Many of the stories and sayings I quote in this book come from the *Apophthegmata Patrum* (*The Sayings of the Desert Fathers*) and from those who have studied them.

For the first three hundred years of the church, Christianity was spreading amidst persecution and hardship, but in the reign of the Roman emperor Constantine the Great, it became the

official faith of the Roman Empire. Constantine himself converted to Christianity in AD 312. His reasons are debated: Was it
a political move, or was his adoption of the faith genuine? Either
way, in AD 313 he issued the Edict of Milan, stopping the persecution of the Christian faith. In AD 380 Christianity became the
state church of the Roman Empire. It was in this time of great
transition from persecution to tolerance to wide acceptance that
many of the faithful started to move into the desert. Some specu-
late that it was the church losing its way, diluted by the now-
welcoming culture, which led many to retreat into the desert
to pursue total devotion to God. However, before Constantine,
there had already been a slow trickle to this way of life by those
looking to live a more ascetic life in devotion to Christ. As early
as the end of the third century, people began taking to the desert.
Whatever the reasons, by the fourth century, the deserts of Egypt,
Palestine, Syria, and Arabia had become home to thousands of
people seeking God. Some of them lived by themselves as her-
mits in caves; others formed small groups of two to three or large
communes of tens to hundreds and eventually thousands. This is
where the Christian monastic tradition was born.

What thrust thousands of people into the desert was the
endeavor to live lives where God was the King of their whole
beings. It was in the desert that the harsh life of ascetic living waged war upon them; they battled with the darkness of
the world and the weaknesses in themselves. They overcame,

and what emerged has influenced and changed Christianity forever. They responded to God's love and sought to let go of everything else, anything that could distract them. They were left only with themselves and the needs of the body to survive: some food to eat and a place to sleep. They knew there was more of God to be discovered. They hungered and thirsted for God, catching sight of something beautiful and pursuing it: a greater vision of life and our place within it. This all sounds grandiose and glory filled, but practically it looked like hiking into the desert, finding a cave, and forming a rhythm of daily prayer.

The stories give different reasons why individuals ended up in the desert. Some, like Anthony the Great, heard this Scripture in church one day: "If you want to be perfect, go, sell your possessions and give to the poor, and you will have treasure in heaven. Then come, follow me" (Matthew 19:21). He was moved by it and built the rest of his life upon that verse. Others felt a kind of gravity pulling them in, which reminds me of the words following Jesus' baptism in Mark 1:12: "At once the Spirit sent him out into the wilderness." Some fled violence, some vice—their own and the vices of others— though they learnt quickly the desert was not a place of escape but a place of war of the mind and heart. It was not a nice retreat to a pleasant land; it was a massive advancement of the Kingdom of Heaven. Whatever got them there, it seems God was doing something profound. I have found that by looking at the Desert Fathers' understanding of Scripture, their wisdom in acknowledging evil, and their practical application of truth to their lives, I am better equipped for the mission Christ has given me.

It is here that I want to note a caution. When writing about the past, it is easy to romanticize it, to say, "Oh, how good it once was. If we could only go back to their time." We then can find ourselves erecting idols of religious practices, like the monk praying by candlelight or some sort of self-flagellating ascetic life. While we borrow from the past, we need to stay grounded in our own context, being part of Christian community and recognizing God is working today as He did then. Although a lot of the Desert Fathers' practices were quite extreme, and sometimes perhaps involved an unhealthy level of self-denial, I find the heart behind it so inspiring. "They had the hard work and experience of a lifetime of striving to redirect every aspect of body, mind, and soul to God."[3] Their complete devotion and their surrender to Christ seems next to none. While I want to celebrate what has gone before and bring the riches of our Christian history to the modern day, our true faith and spirituality is found in everyday life. It is to the here and now that these teachings must speak. These discoveries in the desert can speak to us wherever we are: at college, with our family, in the workplace. They can help us with our annoying neighbor or our difficult colleague. It is where we meet the world that our faith and what it teaches us can make the greatest impact.

God blessed the Desert Fathers and Mothers with His presence, and the stories and teachings that emerged are fascinating. They always viewed God's presence as a gift of love. They did not set out in search of a spiritual experience; they just wanted to surrender themselves, to offer their lives completely out of their love for God.

In the desert they met God's love for them. Their asceticism and devotion were not the cause of God's love for them—God's love for them was the reason they went. In going, they simply discovered more of this truth. It is not just for them but for us all, to know beyond all doubt that God loves us. I write this book with one simple goal in mind: to help people know they are loved in a world that teaches them that they have to earn it, to bring light into the darkness.

Breathe.

You are loved.
Beloved.

BE STILL

Be still, and know that I am God.

PSALM 46:10

K nowing you are loved is different from experiencing it. Both are key, though we as humans tend to trust more in our feelings than in our knowledge. We therefore go after the emotional experience of God more than simply being with God. Too often, we seek the hand of God's blessing rather than the beauty of His face. Both of these are good, but they are often accessed differently. I hope that at some point in your life you have experienced the overwhelming love that God has for you, that you have felt His hand of blessing upon you and been embraced by His presence. Sometimes we might experience a sense of love in worship. Sometimes we are affected by an event we experience, and God reveals Himself in and through it. Or sometimes it happens as we read the Bible:

something jumps off the page and hits us in a fresh way. At other times we can bump into God's love. It's like all of a sudden our heart expands, and we feel surprised by love while walking down the street. Or at times of pain and trial, suddenly we are aware that God is, in fact, with us.

I remember experiencing God's love one particular time when I was living in Tanzania. We had a nurse working for the mission. She was friendly and got on well with some of the students and pastors. It was brought to my attention, however, that she had been struck off by the medical profession for some incident, and it was in fact illegal for us to be giving her a job. I had to end her contract with us, but I didn't want to expose her to ridicule among the students and pastors so I didn't tell them why I had to do it. From their point of view, I was getting rid of a decent nurse for no reason, and everyone turned on me. Pastors I counted as close friends said I was not acting in a Christian way. There was a lot of hurtful gossip, and I felt alone, isolated and vulnerable. I was only twenty-one. I prayed to God earnestly throughout that time. I remember praying an odd prayer, but it came from deep within me: "Father, I am Your son, and I need a hug from You." I fell asleep. In my dream I was lying on the ground, and a circle of people were surrounding me. They were praying for me. Then a person came forward, picked me up, and embraced me. It was so healing. My body filled with love, and my worry and anxiety left. I woke up and read Genesis 8:11: "When the dove returned to him in the evening, there in its beak was a freshly plucked olive leaf! Then Noah knew that the water had receded from the earth." I knew this situation, although great, would now pass, and it did.

A dream is certainly one way we can experience God's love. We feel it, and it is good. But feelings eventually fade and become memories. There is a hard truth here: these feelings and their memory can't sustain a lifelong walk of faith. They help, but they cannot be the only thing we rely on. It can be so encouraging to look back at these moments in our faith journey when God spoke to us or when we experienced something profound. But we must root them in a truth deeper than our emotions: the knowledge that we are loved by God. This knowledge is what faith is. While it may be based on experience, emotion is not its fuel. Faith's fuel comes from a belief in the fundamental truth that we are loved, which experiences with God can support but do not determine. Knowing this truth at our deepest level is the place I believe God wants us to get to. This is faith: to be able to praise God in the darkness, to trust Him in the chaos, to hold to Him in a raging storm because through it all you know you are loved.

One of my favorite passages of Scripture is "be still, and know that I am God" (Psalm 46:10). I love that it doesn't say, "Be still and think about me" or "Be still and believe in me." It says *know.*

"Be still, and know that I am God."

Let go of doubt for a moment.

Simply be silent.

Know that God is with you—that He loves you.

It is within the silence—away from experience—that we get to the deeper place of knowing we are loved.

One Desert Father who spoke about silence was Arsenius the Great. He was born in Rome in AD 354, a well-educated man of senatorial rank. He had wealth and status, but he eventually left it all and went to the desert:

> While still living in the palace, Abba Arsenius prayed to God in these words, "Lord, lead me in the way of salvation." And a voice came saying to him, "Arsenius, flee from men and you will be saved."
>
> Having withdrawn to the solitary life he made the same prayer again and he heard a voice saying to him, "Arsenius, flee, be silent, pray always, for these are the source of sinlessness."[1]

This story speaks to me about the way God encouraged this holy man to seek Him, to turn to silence and prayer and not to base his life around people, possessions, and events. He could have chosen to let his money and power define him. But God called him away from it all, to flee and find silence. It was in this place that he could perceive the only true voice he would need. Seeking to hear the voice of God above all other voices was a goal of the Desert Fathers. There is a universal call for all of us here: Christianity stands apart from all other faiths and world ideals in that it says your identity is received and not earned. You are loved and of value regardless of what you have done or not done. Have you heard this? Are you listening for God's voice? Are you spending time in silence and prayer so you can hear that whisper?

When was the last time you intentionally entered into silence? What I mean is, when have you taken the time to sit down in place—perhaps in a room with the door shut—closed your eyes, and remained still? The Greek Orthodox Church has a wonderful theology on the work of the Holy Spirit and prayer. I have studied it a little, and one thing I have picked up is this: as birds fly and fish swim, a person prays. Something uniquely human is our capacity to pray. By our very nature, we are able to be in communion with God. Many traditional Orthodox churches have no seats, as standing upright on two legs is our natural position as humans and standing still in silence is an act of prayer. All we need to do is be aware of God, and we are in prayer.

Learning silence is an odd thing. Sometimes we can enter

easily: we sit down, take a breath, and like a blanket thrown over us, we surrender to it and we're in. But other times it is like trying to catch a squirrel: our mind flits and rushes about. Training and practicing silence does help, but honestly not always. You may have been doing it for years and still find times when it feels like you're trying to hold oil or catch smoke. Similarly, you may do it for the first time and suddenly find a profound sense of internal stillness.

I have always appreciated having a designated space in which to think on God and pray. In our previous home I made a little "chapel" in a small room. I would go in there to pray. In our current house I have a chair in my study set apart for quiet time, time to pray and be still. There is something innate in humans that hungers for the divine, to be present with God. We are made for it. In a world of distraction and noise, we need to rediscover the wealth of silence. For in this place, we receive who we are and find our worth—not because of the act of silence but because the act allows us to receive. It is active and passive at the same time; we still our bodies and engage our spirit.

Breathe.

Where is your silent place?

———— ✠ ————

Simply put, there are two types of silence: interior and exterior. Interior silence, the quiet calm in ourselves, is helped by exterior silence but not always reliant on it. My wife was once in a counseling session where they were practicing some relaxation breathing exercises, but the counselor's office was right next to a school, and the playground was full of kids running around screaming and yelling. It was hard for her to find the inward silence as her mind kept focusing on the noise. Life can feel a little bit like this sometimes. The world was perhaps easier to quiet down before technology. We could simply walk away from people. But now we all have our devices stuck to us. If it's not an iPhone in our pocket, it's an Apple Watch on our wrist. People can now sometimes go on specifically digital-free retreats to get away from it all. Jesus often went to solitary places to pray or asked His disciples to wait somewhere while He went a little farther ahead to pray, as in the garden of Gethsemane. Following His baptism, He went into the desert for an extended period for silence and prayer. He recognized too when His disciples were tired and needed silence, and He tried to take them away with Him (for example, see Mark 6:31). It's not just about finding a quiet place for prayer; it's about quieting ourselves. There are many ways to pray, and while the most commonly understood way is to talk to God out loud or in our heads, there is also a time to be still and focus on being present with God without words.

The world has never been so "connected" and in contact as it is now. Historically, the invention of the printing press changed the world, as information could be rapidly copied and transported. Ever since then, communication technology has developed by leaps and bounds. The year 2007 marked another milestone in world history, the birth of a new era, with the release of the iPhone and the new popularity of Twitter and Facebook. One effect was that the world got louder and perhaps distraction became the greatest tool of the devil. We desperately need to rediscover the joy and power of silence.

"The first requirement for prayer is silence. People of prayer are people of silence."[2] This phrase is commonly attributed to Mother Teresa of Calcutta, that amazing woman of faith. Silence has long been part of our Christian tradition and is still practiced throughout the world in all the monastic traditions, yet this way to communicate with God is often neglected in our churches, to our detriment.

Meditate on this: You are a miracle. You were formed from the earth and then given life by God's own breath. His Spirit was breathed into you. Your very being is a manifestation of the glory of God to the glory of God.

Know this: it is in silence that we can begin to know this deep and eternal connection. This is what it means to become human: after knowing and practicing these truths and experiencing God's love through our prayer and silence, we begin to share in this love with those around us. We start living in a way affected by what we now know and feel about ourselves. We give, serve, sacrifice. We become like Christ in this world as we show His love to the world. When this happens, we become what we were made for: we truly become human.

Practical Help with Silence

1. Find a place to sit, somewhere in your house or close by where you can visit easily.

2. Sit with your back straight, feet planted on the ground, and hands on your lap open or facing down. The key is comfort.

3. Take a deep breath, slowly exhale, and welcome the Holy Spirit.

4. Say, "Jesus" or "Abba," or pray a short prayer like this one, known as the Jesus prayer: "Lord Jesus Christ, Son of God, have mercy on me, a sinner." Then just be in the moment.

5. When thoughts arise, observe them. Let them go; don't engage. Sit on the bank of your mind and let the

thoughts, like ships, sail by. If you find you are getting distracted by something and perhaps engaging with a thought, say the word or prayer again and start over. If there is a thought or a big concern, like a ship parked in your mind that won't seem to sail by, just let it be. Observe that it is there. You don't need to sort it out right now; just come back to your word or prayer and be on the bank with God.

If you can manage five or ten minutes, that is great. From there you can build to more, eventually tapping into the deeper silence within you on walks, buses, trains, or wherever.

You are beloved!

That is the profound truth that you can learn to know about yourself. That's your identity. Cling to that. Now, in the next section, let's turn to explore how that love is expressed in the exterior world in which we live.

PART 2

FOR GOD
SO LOVED
THE WORLD

7

OPEN MY EYES

God dwells in His creation and is everywhere indivisibly

present in all His works.... He is transcendent above all

His works even while He is immanent within them.

A. W. TOZER, *The Pursuit of God*

The world is really a beautiful place.

Not too long ago, since I have had over ten years in ministry, I was given three months' sabbatical to travel, pray, and write. My wife and I were discussing where to go for a big family trip during this time off, and an American friend said if you could go anywhere in the world, then why not go to the island of Maui in Hawaii. After saving up and planning, we went. I remember sitting on the golden sand of a beautiful beach as the sun was setting in a vibrant red sky. My girls were giggling and playing in the shallows, escaping and chasing the waves as they ebbed and flowed up and down the beach. Humpback whales were breaching in front of us, giving out these great, exhaling bursts as it was whale season, and a couple of sea turtles were bobbing to our right. It was breathtaking. I had to take a moment and felt myself exclaim, "Wow!" I thought heaven could not be far off from this. I was surrounded by beauty.

Perhaps you have had one of those moments of awe in nature that simply strip you back to a childlike state and you go, "Wow!" There is something in the created world that speaks to us, without words, into our souls.

When was the last time you said, "Wow" in awe?

I wonder if you ever saw the video posted by the "double-rainbow guy," Paul "Bear" Vasquez, on YouTube.[1] Sadly he has passed now, but his reaction to a double rainbow in the sky is quite incredible and moving and has been viewed over fifty million times. If you haven't seen the clip, look it up. In that short video, this man was able to highlight and capture something beautiful. He reacts in an uninhibited way that, though it might at first seem strange, actually rings true. He shouts, moans, and weeps at the beauty before him, and it is a wonder to watch. His response to nature, while being quite ecstatic, feels very human. Perhaps that's why so many people have watched the video.

It is not uncommon for people to come to faith all of a sudden when experiencing the beauty of creation. I knew a guy years back who told me this happened to a girl whom he had been praying would find God. She was out walking one day in the English countryside and suddenly experienced a moment of divine beauty. I don't have the details of the story, unfortunately, but I know she was an atheist when she left on the walk and was a believer when she returned. She experienced something of God speaking into her heart through the creation around her all at once and unexpectedly. My friend who described it to me said this girl just realized in that moment that God was real. In a parable about the Kingdom of Heaven in Matthew 13:44, Jesus talks about a man who stumbles upon a treasure in a field. The idea is that all of a sudden someone discovers Christ almost by accident, and everything is changed. I love that image.

I live in London but occasionally head back to where I grew up and where my parents still live. Their home backs onto farmland, and I love walking my parents' dogs in the countryside. I have had moments out walking when the sun breaks through the clouds and lights up a field or some other beautiful scene, and it's like the curtain of heaven has been pulled back for a moment and I'm engulfed in the beauty of it. I find myself praying so much more easily at these times. It just comes out of me.

Where are the places you find it easy to pray?

Perhaps the single greatest moment that reveals God's love and care for His creation is the Incarnation: God becoming one of us.

The Scriptures are dedicated to helping each of us enter into this amazing moment that changed all of human history. As John records in his Gospel's opening, "The Word became flesh and dwelt among us" (1:14, esv). God became man, showing in that moment the worth of creation. It is not that suddenly creation found worth, but that moment shows the worth God always saw in the created world. Why did Christ come? Was it to defeat the works of the devil and defeat sin? Yes, of course it was. But Franciscans also insist on what they call "the primacy of Christ," which they see taught in Scripture. Simply put, the primacy of Christ means that God intended to enter creation from the beginning—it wasn't just a backup plan to deal with sin. John Duns Scotus, who was a great Franciscan theologian, based his ideas about Christ's primacy on various Scriptures, including Ephesians 1:4-5: "That is, in Christ, he chose us before the world was made so that we would be his holy people—people without blame before him. Because of his love, God had already decided to make us his own children through Jesus Christ. That was what he wanted and what pleased him" (ncv).

God always intended to reveal Himself to us through Jesus, to show us His love, and to bring us to Himself. The primary reason that Jesus came to earth, that God became flesh, was not only to provide a solution for our sin; it was also because of God's love for all that He had made. He loved us and wanted us to know His love, and He wanted to make us holy by showing us the way to Him. Jesus' mission was to bring us into a loving relationship with the Father through His life and His teaching. He revealed the true character of God in the world and in His ultimate revelation of God's love: laying down His life for us. Jesus was not born to simply die; He was born to show us in His life that God is with us. He died not only for our sins but to show us the extent of God's love for us. The Franciscan teaching is that we shouldn't link Jesus' coming to sin alone. Some would go further and say that if the reason for the Incarnation is sin, that is blasphemy! The argument is that it would lessen Jesus to partner the wonder of the Incarnation with the negative of sin. Another way of looking at it is if you only associate Jesus' coming with our sin, you could by logic reach the conclusion that it would be better if Jesus had never come, as it would signify that we didn't sin and therefore didn't need Him! Jesus was always going to come into this world. The tearing of the curtain in the Temple, as recorded in Matthew 27:51, signifies the destruction of the separation of God's children from His presence. Jesus has in His life revealed God to us, as if God steps out of the Holy of Holies to His people and then in His death destroys the curtain which separated us from Him. His sacrifice and defeat of sin is part of His mission but not the totality of it. Jesus was born to show us the fullest revelation of God's love for us by manifesting Himself among His creation—showing His love with His presence, His teaching, and His miracles, and then ultimately making a way for us to enter God's presence through His death on the cross. Why? Because we are beloved!

Breathe.

The curtain has been torn.
God is with us, and we can be with God.
We stand in awe.

The apostle Paul writes, "Since the creation of the world God's invisible qualities—his eternal power and divine nature—have been clearly seen, being understood from what has been made, so that people are without excuse" (Romans 1:20). Basically, no one can say they don't know something of God, as creation all around us communicates about Him. Now let's move from the special revelation of Jesus as God with us, to the general revelation of God revealing Himself through His creation. This is not a novel idea in the New Testament. It is part of the whole scriptural narrative. Let's look at the first half of Psalm 19:

The heavens declare the glory of God;

 the skies proclaim the work of his hands.

Day after day they pour forth speech;

 night after night they reveal knowledge.

They have no speech, they use no words;

 no sound is heard from them.

Yet their voice goes out into all the earth,

 their words to the ends of the world.

In the heavens God has pitched a tent for the sun.

 It is like a bridegroom coming out of his chamber,

 like a champion rejoicing to run his course.

It rises at one end of the heavens

 and makes its circuit to the other;

 nothing is deprived of its warmth.

PSALM 19:1-6

This is a beautiful description of God's wonder and glory being manifested in creation. The psalmist is saying that creation "pour[s] forth speech" and "reveal[s] knowledge" about God's nature and character. We, as the crown of creation, need only to pay attention, to have an open heart and open eyes to see and allow creation to speak to us about God.

Our Christian story is one of creation and re-creation. God did not create everything and then leave it to its own end, but He is constantly in the process of re-creating everything, as Psalm 19 indicates. Our view of the created order around us needs to be informed by our knowledge that God is intimately involved with all that He created, not separated from it. This isn't an essay on why you should recycle. But do realize the tall trees, the bright-blue skies, the serene seas are all part of God's vehicle of communicating love to you. The world around us is part of His self-revelation. When we treat the world with no regard, we are rejecting and injuring God's love—like turning away from a lover's kiss.

Breathe.

Lord, open my heart.
Open my eyes . . . to Your beauty.

WAKE UP TO WONDER

In everything beautiful he saw him, who is beauty
itself, and he followed his beloved everywhere
by his likeness imprinted on creation.

BROTHER RAMON, *Franciscan Spirituality*

Doesn't St. Francis of Assisi appear to be the patron saint of birdbaths? Think about it. If you see him depicted, it is quite often in a church garden or retreat house immortalized in statue form surrounded by animals, whether doves, rabbits, or a wolf as a birdbath. Frankly, I wouldn't mind a Franciscan birdbath in my garden, though many of my friends would cringe. That might be one of my reasons for wanting one!

Francis, of course, loved animals and creation. It was common for him to burst out in rapturous praise while walking with his brothers in the fields around Assisi. In one funny story I once heard Francis runs to the church in the center of town in the middle of the night and manically rings the church bell, which was usually a sign of an invading army or some news of tremendous import. When the townspeople gathered to see what was happening, he shouted to them, "Have you seen the moon tonight? Look at how big and beautiful it is!"[1] I can't help but giggle to myself at what the people must have thought.

On more than one occasion, one of my daughters has picked up a big leaf and handed it to me saying, "Wow! Daddy, look—a leaf!" Kind of silly, I know. But there is something there about the humility to be amazed by simple beauty.

Have we lost this?

Go out into nature and discover God again in its beauty.
Stand in the rain and know God is present.
Sense God's great power echoed in a thunderstorm.
See God's handiwork as He raises the sun or sets it to bed.
Wake up to wonder.

Breathe.

Creation, of course, is brutal too. There is no getting away from that: packs of wolves that devour the weak deer, earthquakes that destroy homes and break up families. Creation needs redemption and restoration too. The Bible promises that death and destruction will fade away in the new heaven and new earth. We will get to that shortly. But here I want to encourage you that you don't need to be afraid of falling into error when thinking about creation and its wonder. As Francis did, simply glorify the Creator—not the creation. Let the earth's beauty and power lead you to praise the One who made it. The road of your life can be focused on discovering God again and again through all of His creation.

———————— ✛ ————————

Stand in the rain.
Take in a sunset.
Walk barefoot on the grass.
Recognize how all of this can communicate
something of God's glory to you.
Wake up to wonder.

Breathe.

———————— ✛ ————————

It takes my breath away how Communion is rooted in the earthiness of creation. Jesus takes bread and calls it His body. He holds a cup of wine and calls it His blood. Jesus uses elements of the earth itself to symbolize His own body. Spend some time rediscovering the deep mystery of Communion. There is much I could say about this, but for now I'll say these few words:

Taste and see that God is good.

In the Eucharistic liturgy, which we use in the Church of England and is also used in other denominations, there is an option to say the following as the minister prepares the bread and wine. It is called prayers of preparation of the table.

Priest: Blessed are you, Lord God of all creation: through your goodness we have this bread to set before you, which earth has given and human hands have made. It will become for us the bread of life.

    People: Blessed be God forever.

    Priest: Blessed are you, Lord God of all creation: through your goodness we have this wine to set before you, fruit of the vine and work of human hands. It will become for us the cup of salvation.

    People: Blessed be God forever.[2]

Receiving Communion is arguably the greatest act of worship that we can offer, as it celebrates the greatest act of worship *ever* offered: Jesus dying on a cross in obedience to the Father's will. This all involves creation: us eating and drinking of the bread and wine and the One who created it, the Word made flesh, Jesus.

———————◈———————

Taste and see that God is good.
Wake up to wonder.

Breathe.

GOD LOVES THE WORLD

For God so loved the world that he gave his one and only Son.

JOHN 3:16

I n the UK we have many old churches. They are beautiful and can inspire awe, but they can also be a great burden to maintain. The heating, the roof, the gutters, the windows, the bell tower, the brickwork, and even the foundation can all have issues due to age. In fact, as a vicar I have had problems at my church in each of these areas apart from the foundation, thank God. My church, St. Saviour's Wendell Park, is not that old by UK standards. It was built in 1894 and was known as "the church in the fields," as when it was created it was surrounded by fields. Now it is in a built-up residential area in West London. When I first came to the church, it was struggling. It hadn't had a vicar for over two years. There were only about twelve people who would regularly worship, and these faithful people were exhausted trying to keep the lights on and the doors open. At the front of the church there was a garden, if you could call it that. It was overgrown and acted like a screen to the building. Untended bushes and large trees hid the face of the church. People would use it as a toilet and dumping ground. Quite early on, I wanted to work on this. As people went past the church, they saw an unkempt, unloved building that looked like it was being swallowed up. This image was a symbol that somehow spoke about what was going on inside. We decided to clear it out and make a garden where people could sit and children could play. One of our members kindly gave some money, and we went to work. The area was transformed: the weeds were pulled, the bushes trimmed and taken out. We built a flower bed and put in paving stones. We trimmed back a rosebush but left it in the middle of the small garden. It took work, it took effort, but the result was great. It was amazing to see, and once this dark canopy was lifted, lots of bluebells and flowers that we didn't know existed bloomed in spring. The rosebush, now not strangled by other plants, burst into color, and countless roses emerged. It is interesting to note that inside the church, our congregation started to grow too. New families and individuals came, some who used to come but had drifted away came back, and the church tripled in size quite quickly. Sometimes the physical world reflects something that is going on in the spiritual world.

Have you ever noticed that the curse in the Genesis story is a curse of the land? The land will produce thorns and thistles:

> To Adam [God] said, "Because you listened to
> your wife and ate fruit from the tree about which
> I commanded you, 'You must not eat from it,'
>
> "Cursed is the ground because of you;
>> through painful toil you will eat food from it
>> all the days of your life.
> It will produce thorns and thistles for you,
>> and you will eat the plants of the field."
>
> GENESIS 3:17-18

This idea is mirrored at the crucifixion of Jesus when a crown of thorns is made and placed on His head and He is dressed in a purple robe. This has been seen to signify the thorns and the purple flowers of thistles. As we read in John 19:1-2, "Then Pilate took Jesus and had him flogged. The soldiers twisted together a crown of thorns and put it on his head. They clothed him in a purple robe."

God was not just redeeming *us* on the cross; He was redeeming all of His creation, the fallenness of all things. John 3:16, a verse that is sometimes referred to as the gospel in miniature, says, "For God so loved the world that he gave his one and only Son, that whoever believes in him shall not perish but have eternal life."

The Greek word translated "world" in this passage is κόσμον or *kosmon*. This can be used to describe the world, the universe or the cosmos, worldly affairs, or the inhabitants of the world. This verse is saying God loves all of creation, the universe and everyone in it. Then comes the second part of the verse, appealing directly to humanity, the crown of His creation, to believe in His salvific work. We are part of creation being saved by God, but we are not the only part being saved.

This is why the natural world itself turns to praise God too. The passage below speaks to this all-encompassing redemption, as the briers and thistles become juniper and myrtle:

As the rain and the snow
  come down from heaven,
and do not return to it
  without watering the earth
and making it bud and flourish,
    so that it yields seed for the sower and bread for
      the eater,
so is my word that goes out from my mouth:

It will not return to me empty,

but will accomplish what I desire

　　and achieve the purpose for which I sent it.

You will go out in joy

　　and be led forth in peace;

the mountains and hills

　　will burst into song before you,

and all the trees of the field

　　will clap their hands.

Instead of the thornbush will grow the juniper,

　　and instead of briers the myrtle will grow.

This will be for the LORD's renown,

　　for an everlasting sign,

　　that will endure forever.

ISAIAH 55:10-13

Doesn't this set your heart aflame for God? Doesn't this root you back to the wonderful creation from which your form was made? This recognition of the goodness and beauty of creation—and that we are part of it—brings a smile to my soul. Thorn and thistle will yield to life-giving trees. Nature itself will be redeemed. This is one of the things that I have found so inspiring in the teaching of St. Francis of Assisi. Here is a section from his famous "Canticle of Creatures," which puts it well:

Praised be You, my Lord, with all Your creatures,
especially Sir Brother Sun,
Who is the day and through whom You give us light.
And he is beautiful and radiant with great splendor;
and bears a likeness of You, Most High One.

Praised be You, my Lord, through Sister Moon and
the stars,
in heaven You formed them clear and precious
and beautiful.

Praised be You, my Lord, through Brother Wind,
and through the air, cloudy and serene, and
every kind of weather,
through whom You give sustenance to Your creatures.[1]

I hope that you can let the words of Francis help you appreciate how much God is communicating through nature. I believe if you allow God to, He will speak to you through the created order around you, whether it is a birdsong you hear when you are worried about something or the beauty of a tree as its leaves turn color and drop away. He is the Creator of both you and the nature around you. We are both being redeemed for something better.

———————— ✠ ————————

Take a break from our tech-saturated world and go outside.

Breathe the air.

Feel the sun.

Listen to the wind in the trees and the songs of the birds.

God speaks through His creation.

Breathe.

PART 3

THE

DEEPEST

YOU

—————— ✛ ——————

BE FREE

Daughter, your faith has healed you. Go in
peace and be freed from your suffering.

During the pandemic, when we could meet with only one person outside, I started going on long walks around London with my brother-in-law. One time we walked for thirty-two kilometers. We walked along the River Thames and past historic buildings and landmarks like St. Paul's Cathedral and the Houses of Parliament. The streets were eerily empty of people. It was strange to see London like this. As we walked, we talked about all kinds of things. On one occasion, we were walking along a road with large, beautiful houses on each side of us, approaching Hyde Park, when we came across a man kneeling face down on the path. It was striking and strange to see this man, who was dressed quite normally, in a curled-up position, on his knees with his head on the ground in front of him. For a moment I thought he might be praying, but as we approached, it struck me that he could be in trouble.

I asked him if he was okay, and he said, "Yes, please don't touch me. I have a chronic back problem, and I need to do this for twenty minutes. I'll be fine. Thanks, guys." He was obviously in great pain, but we carried on.

In Mark 5, Jesus heals a hemorrhaging woman, and Scripture tells us she is "freed from her suffering" (verse 29). For the man I encountered on a London street, being freed from suffering would mean having his back healed and being released from physical pain. Even though we were total strangers, I could see his physical suffering. But who knows the suffering he had that I couldn't see? Perhaps he was married and had kids but couldn't carry them, perhaps he loved sport but could no longer play, or perhaps he hadn't had a good night's sleep for years.

We don't all suffer from physical ailments, but all of us live with hurts of some kind. Maybe we have a rocky relationship with a spouse or a parent, or maybe we experienced trauma early in life. Surely the idea of being freed from suffering includes this kind of thing too.

What would it mean for you to be freed from your suffering?

The truth is that we all have issues.

I carry pain from school, from my parents, from past relationships. In the New Testament, miracle-healing stories can often be thought of as just physical: the man born blind getting his sight, the mute tongue speaking, or the paraplegic being able to walk. These are amazing, of course! But, as a pastor, the big issues people bring to me, and which they are seeking healing for, are usually not physical. Not a broken leg, but a broken soul.

I have had countless conversations with people who are so lost that they wish they were no longer here. One person recently told me that they wish they would just have a quick death. Another said to me that they saw so many people die needlessly, and it was such a waste when they would happily take their place. This didn't come from a healthy way of thinking. They had lost all sense of their own value. They were in great pain, but this pain wasn't physical. It was on a deeper level. Often, people need support from mental health professionals when they find themselves in this place, and I point them in that direction. But I also believe that Jesus is God and that God longs to meet us in our need—whether physical, emotional, or spiritual—and bring us healing.

In the story from Mark 5, Jesus doesn't just heal the hemorrhaging woman physically. She receives emotional and spiritual healing too. For me, this is one of the most inspiring healing stories in the whole Bible. Jesus has just arrived back on the shores of Galilee in the area of Capernaum. There, crowds gather to see and hear Him. Within the crowd is a woman who has suffered bleeding for twelve years. She has tried in every way to get better, but she has not experienced healing. Yet in the midst of her great suffering, there is still health in her faith! She thinks, *If I can just touch Jesus' cloak, I will be healed.*

> When she heard about Jesus, she came up behind
> him in the crowd and touched his cloak, because she
> thought, "If I just touch his clothes, I will be healed."
> Immediately her bleeding stopped and she felt in her
> body that she was freed from her suffering.
>
> MARK 5:27-29

In this miracle story, there is more going on than physical healing. Jesus also restores the woman to the community that rejected her. He heals the wounds of her relationship with God, whom she might have thought had abandoned her, and reminds her of who she is. Jesus calls her a daughter and commends her faith. He frees her from shame.

We all feel shame at certain points in our lives. It's one of the most powerful negative emotions there is. Guilt says, *I did something bad.* Shame says, *I am bad.* Shame is intimate and therefore very powerful as it whispers lies about who we are at our core. Shame is the swampland of the soul. It will keep us wet, cold, and trapped. It's like a universal straitjacket. It limits us. It's the voice that says, *You're dirty. You're bad. You're not enough. You're fooling no one. You're a mistake.* It's the voice that says the real you is the hidden, sordid, addicted mess of your inner battles. The bits no one sees.

We all feel shame to some degree in different ways. Sometimes this can come from personal experiences and sometimes from voices in the culture we grow up in. Sometimes the voice of shame can hold up an ideal and compare you against it. It can say that you should be all kinds of things or feel certain feelings about your life and what you should do. These messages may set up unrealistic expectations or standards.

In my experience of pastoring, and based on what I see online, I've noticed that women often feel pressure to be a kind of goddess: to excel at work, be successful, have a family, run the house, organize the kids' education and medical requirements, achieve an athletic physique, and do all of this with ease.

One of the major voices I feel—and I think other men often feel too—is the voice which says, *Do not be weak or perceived as weak.* This can mean different things to different people. In me, the voice is loudest when I feel overlooked or pushed aside, when I'm not taken seriously. I heard once that men often go to the doctor and say, "I'm struggling with anger" when they are actually depressed. It's as if anger and aggression are more manly emotions than feeling sad or depressed, which they think reveals weakness.

The feeling of shame limits us and can stop people from reaching out for the help they need. We feel like we should be a certain way, and if we're not, then we must be either weak or worthless. A lot of people want to avoid admitting their struggles because they are afraid other people will forever see them as weak and expect less of them in general.

But there is strength in admitting our struggles.

Growing up, I carried a lot of shame. I was known as bad—a naughty child. Of course sometimes I did naughty things, but I was also an extrovert. I was a loud and exuberant character. I was also a twin, so there were two of us. For some people, we were a lot to handle. Sometimes it was bad behavior, and sometimes it was just my personality! There is a distinction between our actions and who we are. At school I remember being reminded of how stupid I was, how bad I was. At university, a very low period of my life, I remember feeling weak, and I hated myself because of my perceived weaknesses. The feeling of *I am bad* is something I had to battle with—and still do.

When I have talked to people who have suffered at the hands of someone, whether a bully or an abusive partner, often the person they are most angry with is themselves. It might be because they feel weak and hate themselves for what, in their view, they *allowed* to be done to them. This is a lie that comes from shame. We all have lies that shame whispers to us and that we can easily believe about ourselves.

The antidote to shame is empathy. There is true and powerful empathy in Jesus. Let's return to the story of the hemorrhaging woman in Mark 5. Jesus meets this woman while He is on the way to the house of Jairus, whose daughter is ill. Jairus, a synagogue leader, a man with great respect and a high position among the people in the area, has come to Jesus and fallen at His feet in front of the crowd and begged Him to come heal his twelve-year-old daughter. This was a risky thing for Jairus to do because the gospel story has already described how other religious leaders were plotting against Jesus. Jesus goes with Jairus, and the story of the hemorrhaging woman comes as a kind of interruption to the story of Jairus and his daughter.

I love how much of Jesus' ministry comes from interruptions to a journey somewhere else. God is often in the interruptions.

At the time, the hemorrhaging woman would have been seen as not only unwell but unclean. The Jewish people had strict purity laws which were taken very seriously. There were rules about which foods were considered clean or unclean. There were rules about Jewish people associating with Gentile (non-Jewish) people. A lot of things could make someone unclean. On the list was a menstruating woman. There's a section in

Leviticus 15 which talks in detail about this being a time when women were considered ceremonially unclean. Anything a woman touched would become ceremonially unclean as well.

The hemorrhaging woman would not have been allowed into the Temple. She would not have been able to go to that holy place and worship her God. This woman had been bleeding for twelve years! She would not have been able to go to the Temple for twelve years! Her society would have perceived her as cut off from God—and she may have *felt* cut off from God.

There must have been great shame in being called unclean for so long. This woman was shame personified. She had spent everything she had on medical help and had not gotten better. In coming to Jesus, she may have had to hide herself so that no one would recognize her as part of the jostling crowd. But what does Jesus do? After she touches Him, He knows power has gone out from Him, and He stops in the middle of the crowd. Among all these people, He calls out for the person who touched Him. This must have been pretty scary for her.

When I was a teenager, I had a job in tele-sales, and on my first day I didn't make any sales. At the end of the day, the floor manager gathered everyone together and called out the names of the four people—including me—who hadn't sold anything. It was a culture of shame. Needless to say, I left the job!

Perhaps, in the Mark 5 passage, the woman expected that Jesus would call out her actions and shame her for making Him unclean by touching Him. He was, after all, walking with the synagogue leader, who would have stopped her if she'd tried to enter the synagogue. She comes forward, trembling with fear, and throws herself at His feet. She is the second person in this passage to throw themselves at Jesus' feet. One "clean" synagogue leader and one "unclean" woman. But Jesus does not compare them. He looks at the woman and says, "Daughter, your faith has healed you" (Mark 5:34).

What Jesus does here is quite amazing. He honors the woman in front of everyone. He affirms her value as a daughter, someone precious, someone loved. Probably this had the implication of "a daughter of Abraham," reminding her of her ancestry and her link to the heart of the Jewish people. He declares the value of her faith even though she hadn't been able to formally worship God for years and would have been perceived as having no relationship with God. Her faith is the thing that Jesus calls out as of great value. Genesis 15:6 says, "Abram believed the LORD, and he credited it to him as righteousness." In one short sentence, Jesus has connected the woman to Abraham, commended her strong faith, and implied her righteousness before God—all in front of her community and her synagogue leader. The passage goes on like this:

While Jesus was still speaking, some people came from the house of Jairus, the synagogue leader. "Your daughter is dead," they said. "Why bother the teacher anymore?"

Overhearing what they said, Jesus told him, "Don't be afraid; just believe."

He did not let anyone follow him except Peter, James and John the brother of James. When they came to the home of the synagogue leader, Jesus saw a commotion, with people crying and wailing loudly. He went in and said to them, "Why all this commotion and wailing? The child is not dead but asleep." But they laughed at him.

After he put them all out, he took the child's father and mother and the disciples who were with him, and went in where the child was. He took her by the hand and said to her, *"Talitha koum!"* (which means "Little girl, I say to you, get up!"). Immediately the girl stood up and began to walk around (she was twelve years old). At this they were completely astonished. He gave strict orders not to let anyone know about this, and told them to give her something to eat.

MARK 5:35-43

In both stories Jesus brings healing. He doesn't make a distinction between the "unclean" woman and the "clean" daughter of a synagogue leader. He helps them both. In fact, He stops and helps the bleeding woman; He doesn't make her wait until after He's seen the clean daughter.

There is no hierarchy to the love of God.

All are loved equally as daughters and sons.

It is interesting that Jesus only took the parents and Peter, James, and John with Him when He went to the house where Jairus's daughter was. He didn't make a spectacle to amaze the crowd; He healed a family. He was totally present with them. Jesus was always doing things in a way that people weren't expecting and turning things upside down. The wealthy and powerful—as well as the rejected and shamed—will fall at His feet, and He will raise up whoever calls out to Him. Jesus is compassionate and merciful.

He calls us out of our shame and restores us.
He brings healing and a new vision of who we are.
We are His children.
We are loved.

Breathe.

Sometimes the shame we feel is in the secret places of our hearts and minds. The parts that we often hide. We can fall into the lie that these secret places represent our real self, since when we are alone, the voices of shame are the loudest. When we are alone, our thoughts crowd in and our peace is robbed. Sometimes people feel this when they are trying to go to sleep. Sometimes people avoid spending time alone to try to evade those negative whispers. We need to meet the whispered lies we hear with truth.

Truth is not a concept or feeling; truth exists, and we can hold on to it. Jesus is the truth (see John 14:6). He said, "You will know the truth, and the truth will set you free" (John 8:32). Whatever bondage you feel can be broken. The shame that covers you can lift if you know and experience the truth.

This truth is found in Jesus.
Invite Jesus into your thoughts, into your shame,
into the dark places.
He knows about them already.
He can bring healing and restoration.
He can do all things.

Breathe.

Jesus tells us, *I know you, all of you. You are not your weaknesses, your faults, your mistakes. You are Mine, and I died for you because I know the deepest you and it is good.* Jesus draws us out past the jeering crowds, the voices that constantly hound our minds, and calls us children of God. As we read in Psalm 23,

> You prepare a table before me
>> in the presence of my enemies.
> You anoint my head with oil;
>> my cup overflows.
> Surely your goodness and love will follow me
>> all the days of my life,
> and I will dwell in the house of the LORD
>> forever.

PSALM 23:5-6

I love this image, of God taking us by the hand, sitting us down at His table, and honoring us in front of the people who represent the lies we allow ourselves to believe. For me, my enemies are not really people in my daily life but people in my past who, in my memory, correspond to a certain negative voice or feeling. For you, these people might include an oppressive teacher, a bully at school, or an abusive individual at work. They have become a kind of manifestation of whatever lie took root from a past experience. In the midst of all that, God sits us down, honors us, and loves on us.

Our identity is about how God sees us, not how the crowd sees us. If, like the bleeding woman, we focus on Jesus rather than the crowd, we will hear the truth louder.

Jesus will not condemn us when we come to Him. He will not ridicule us. He will not say, "I told you so" or "You got what you deserved." He will love us, accept us, and heal us with His love, because He is love. Shame is a straitjacket, but Christ came for freedom. We are children of God, and we are called to be free from shame. That's why Jesus died for us. He didn't die for the "clean" special ones; He died for us while we were lost in our sin and pinned down by shame. Sometimes our shame also comes out of things that we've done wrong, and we feel that because we've done something bad, we are a bad person. There is nothing that can't be forgiven if you only come to Him and ask.

It's about fresh starts.
He has shown us what He is willing to do for us because He loves
us. Let us encounter the risen Christ again.

Breathe.

I am good and made for good.
I am loved and made for love.

LET GO

Have mercy on me, LORD, for I am faint.

PSALM 6:2

There's an incredible story about St. Francis that I can't forget. I think it's really powerful. One day St. Francis was with Brother Leo, one of his closest friends and fellow monks, in a place where they didn't have their prayer books. Francis was fast becoming known as a "holy man," and his fame had spread. Francis was aware of the trappings that could creep into one's heart if one became famous, and especially for being known as saintly. I think he remembered his early years of revelry and being popular in Assisi, drinking and partying with his friends. He knew the addictive nature of praise and honor—he'd once sought it, and now he feared it could drive him from God if he was not careful. In order to guard himself against the potential sin of pride, Francis suggested to Leo that they say their own liturgy of prayers. He instructed Leo on what to say and told him not to change any words. Francis was trying to get Leo to rebuke him, to point out Francis's sin and condemn him. Francis thought this would keep him humble and be a defense against pride. But Brother Leo, inspired by the Holy Spirit, could not do it. Instead of condemning Francis, as Francis wanted him to do, Brother Leo ended up blessing him:

Francis began. . . . "You have done so many sins and evils in this world, Brother Francis, that you are deserving of hell."

"But God will work through you so much good," Leo replied earnestly, "that surely you will go to paradise."

"No, no, no," Francis said, "that is not right. When I say my part, you must say as I have instructed you, repeating, 'You are worthy only to be set among the cursed in the depths of hell.'"

Again, in obedience, Brother Leo replied, "Willingly, father. I will do it."

This time, Francis paused and painfully considered his words. After a few moments, with tears in his eyes and while pounding his heart, Francis said in a much louder voice: "O Lord of heaven and earth, I have done so much evil and so many sins in this world that I am worthy only to be cursed by you!"

And Leo quickly replied in turn: "O Brother Francis, God will do great things for you and you will be blessed above all others!"

Francis was perplexed and more than a little bit angry.

"Why do you disobey me, Brother Leo? You are to repeat as I have instructed you!"

"God knows, father," Leo answered, "that each time I set my mind to do as you say, God then makes me say what pleases him."

How could Francis argue with this? He marveled at Leo's words, searching them for the divine purpose. Nevertheless, after some time, Francis quietly said, "I pray most lovingly that you will answer me this time as I have asked you to do." Leo agreed to try, but try as he might, again and again, he could not do as Francis wished.[1]

I love this story. St. Francis keeps asking Brother Leo to tell him how terrible he is, and Brother Leo instead replies with how God sees St. Francis, as good and blessed.

Sometimes we think God wants us to spend a lot of time telling Him that we are worthless worms, as though that will please Him or will help us to avoid the sin of pride. But as the story illustrates, the opposite is true. The way to defeat pride is to receive and know God's glorious love. This leads to true humility. Perhaps you have seen people with tattoos on their knuckles: one hand says, "Love" and the other "Hate." The truth is, hate is not the opposite of love—pride is. God's love is not earned; it is given. Acknowledgment of this erodes pride. He doesn't want us to stay in the isolated place of shame, like a child looking at the ground before an angry parent. God wants us to come to Him knowing we are His beloved children. If we can, we will find rest in this place knowing we are loved. From that will come a freer life and a life which is loving towards others. If we find healing, we won't be lashing out from a place of woundedness, and we won't be constantly striving to prove our value to ourselves or others. It is not just that we are loved but also that we were created to be good and show goodness to others. That is what Jesus wants to empower us to do.

Knowing and holding to the foundational truth of our inherent value is a key in the process of dismantling shame. The enemy, it seems, works by whispering lies and reminding us of our mistakes that have left us feeling shame-ridden. We need to replace these destructive thought patterns with positive, true statements. I wonder if, like me, you ever get memories that pop into your mind and actually make you wince. It's as if, for a moment, you were transported back there, and you cringe at what you did or said.

When that happens, follow it up with a truth.

You can't pretend it didn't happen, but you don't have to live under it and have it dictate to you how bad you are. You can remind yourself that you have moved on since then, grown, repented, even forgiven yourself. In these moments, I find it helps to say to myself a simple truth like *I'm loved and I'm forgiven.*

It does you no good to hate yourself and say, *I was no good then, but now I'm better.* I think that is destructive, and it dehumanizes you. Jesus did not hate you when you made these mistakes. Jesus did not die for you because you had it all sorted out. He knew you *didn't*—and He loves you the same. Accept yourself and your weaknesses. That does not mean you say what you did was okay. It means you recognize that your action was wrong, but you have grace and love for yourself. Hold to this foundational truth: you are loved in order to love.

A prayer that might be helpful is *Lord, see my faith in You and not my sin. Help me to hold to You and trust in what You say about me, and help me overcome all that is against me.* The hemorrhaging woman did not allow thoughts of her own unworthiness to hinder her efforts to reach Jesus, though I'm sure she had them. She pushed through them with the single aim of touching Jesus. She came to Him and found healing for herself in more ways than she thought possible.

———————— ✠ ————————

Breathe.

Replace lies with truth.
Meet memories with grace.
Hold tightly to faith in Jesus.
Forgive.
Let go.

PART 4

PEACE
THAT
PASSES
OUR
UNDERSTANDING

✦

WHAT DO YOU
WANT IN LIFE?

Learn the unforced rhythms of grace.

MATTHEW 11:29, MSG

What do you want in life?

It's a pretty straightforward question that is incredibly hard to answer. Most people stutter out an answer like "I want to be happy." There is nothing wrong with wanting to be happy, but happiness is fleeting. It is pleasurable to feel happy, but feelings of happiness are not deep, anchored, or sustainable. My children bring me happiness when they play or laugh or do something surprising, but my feeling for them goes beyond happiness. When I come home after a long day of activity, ring the bell, and hear a little voice cry out, "Daddy's home!" and little feet run to the door, my soul lifts in a way that is greater than happiness. When my youngest daughter falls asleep in the car and I lift her out to transport her to her bed, and she grips around my neck with her little arms and hands and rests her head on my shoulder, it is more than happiness. It is deeper than that. It is love, joy, peace that is in me.

So perhaps a better answer to the question "What do you want in life?" would be "to be loving," "to be joyful," or "to be at peace." I recently came back from a Christian conference that celebrated creativity, and it was great. But there was a sense behind it all of a need to be successful and to be recognized—messages that feed into celebrity culture. The whole experience left me slightly confused in my spirit. I came home early, having had conference fatigue. My brain was full, and I was tired. When I came in the door, my girls jumped on me, and we wrestled around on the floor. It grounded me. It made me reflect that this is precious: family, love, intimacy, and real connection. It made me remember that, in terms of my work, firstly I love being a priest: praying, serving, administering the sacraments. Any successes, fame, or recognition are secondary to the concrete sense of being grounded by love and in love—loving those around me, serving them, and being loved in return. Being in relationship with Jesus is deep, intimate, and fulfilling. My understanding of God as Father feeds me and grounds me. That relationship feels more akin to hanging out with my kids rather than standing on a stage "being successful."

If our anchor is set firm, we can cultivate our emotional state in the proper way and not feel adrift, dependent on circumstance and environment to feed us. Rather, when our souls feed off God, He provides us with an inner source of strength which bubbles up through us, keeping us in peace. In the words of Jesus, "The water I give them will become in them a spring of water welling up to eternal life" (John 4:14). Let me just say, I'm not there yet either! I can't say that I walk around in continual love, joy, and peace, but that doesn't mean I don't believe we can make progress. I do experience more peace, love, and joy than I used to, and I expect to grow in this as my relationship with Jesus develops throughout my life. As I learn to abide in Him more, I will see more of this working its way into my soul, transforming me from the inside out. I know I'm much further along than I used to be, and I am excited about how I can go further in my relationship with Jesus as I look to the future.

But how?

My first bishop in the Kensington area of London said a helpful thing that I come back to now and again: "Define your reality"—not what I would like it to be, but what it actually is. He meant I should be honest and look truthfully out. Sometimes we're not good at this. We believe we have to be happy, full of grace, loving of all. We can form a false reality, one we want or believe we should have rather than what we actually experience. If we stopped and were really honest, we might say, "Actually, I'm stressed out, exhausted, and tired of religion." Eugene Peterson's paraphrase of Jesus' invitation to follow Him begins, "Are you tired? Worn out? Burned out on religion? . . . Walk with me and work with me. . . . Learn the unforced rhythms of grace" (Matthew 11:28-29, MSG).

This is a wonderful teaching. Jesus is not suggesting a list of dos and don'ts. Rather, it seems, He is recognizing that in this world we will bear burdens, and He is saying, "Use My yoke. Be yoked with Me." He is offering equipment for the walk. His yoke is His teaching—His methodology on life, so to speak. For example, His yoke includes His teaching on love, like love your enemies (see Matthew 5:44). It includes His view of judgment—basically don't do it, don't throw the stones (see John 8:7), take the plank from your own eye first (see Matthew 7:3), and sort your heart out (see Luke 6:45). Stop adjusting your behavior and start adjusting your attitude; then your behavior will follow. Reconfigure your understanding of who God is—He is a loving Father who runs to you (see Luke 15:20). Rethink your attitude towards others—serve them (see Matthew 23:11). These are all components of His yoke, and this way of living and being will bring you peace and help you deal with the troubles of life when they come.

It is quite a freeing thought: "Hey, you, it's going to be tough. Use this, and walk with Me—it will help." I love that.

———————— ✠ ————————

In His teaching known as the Sermon on the Mount (see Matthew 5–7), Jesus moves towards a set of principles and more practical lifestyle choices. He gives a kind of manual for being human and how to best live. He recognizes the trials and weaknesses of what it is to be human, talking of sorrow, poverty, and persecution, but He still sets the bar for living very high. He gives out directions—practices, if you like— on how to live: "Love your enemies and pray for those who persecute you" (Matthew 5:44), and so on. When Jesus gives instructions like this, He is describing a person who lives by drawing from that spring within. He is describing Himself, it seems, who prayed for the ones persecuting Him, who loved His enemies, who even laid down His life. Jesus goes on to say, in a sort of summary of His sermon, "Be perfect, therefore, as your heavenly Father is perfect" (verse 48). This is a pretty tough directive—impossible, certainly, in our own strength. This translation, though, is probably a legacy from the Vulgate, which translates the Greek word *teleios* (which can mean "perfect") into Latin as *perfectus* (though even that word doesn't quite have the sense of being without flaws that our English word has).

Although the Greek word *teleios* can mean "perfect," it is more typically used to refer to maturity or wholeness. The word might be better translated as "mature." The impression is to be whole, grounded, and consistently God-centered. This is not a let-off—we will all still struggle here—but it will hopefully help us to better understand what Jesus is communicating here. The call of God is a high one, but His welcome is wide, and Jesus will help us along the way. The main thing is to keep searching God out, keep spending time in prayer, keep letting Him transform us. We will fall short, as the Good Book says, and we need to have grace for ourselves. I'm not what I once was, and not yet what I will be, but I believe that we can grow in holiness as we navigate this life. We can hope for continued sanctification, slowly but surely becoming more Christlike in all we say and do. This transformation in us is the letting go of the kingdoms of this world (money, power, sex, fame, for example) to embrace the coming Kingdom of God.

This Kingdom of God is not a separate geographical place that will present itself one day. Instead, we should see it more as a transforming of what is here, as in our world, ourselves, our environments, a merging of two places into one and a revealing of what God always meant it to be. A simple image I use is to outstretch your fingers on both hands and slowly bring them together, interlocking your fingers. Your hands move towards each other, fingertips crossing first, until your whole hand is interlocked and two hands are one. It's often slow movements that lead to big changes. In our church, this transformation looks like offering a "stay and play" venue for families in the area, where people outside the church come inside and find a warm, safe place to play with their children. We see community form with principles of love and family woven in. Mums and some dads meet and share and chat and sometimes pray for each other in a church setting. It is a small first step towards something greater, like the fingertips coming side by side on their way to interlocking. Another thing we do is support a charity which helps vulnerable adults—whether ex-offenders, homeless people, or refugees—with food or advice or finding work. Again, these are small steps of the Kingdom, helping, loving, serving. Wherever Christians are seen, they will impact their surroundings. Just as a small piece of salt added to food affects the flavor, so we affect our environments by presence and love.

One environment I have been part of for many years is sport. I love sport. I used to play field hockey at a good level, I now play tennis and cricket, and recently I joined a football (soccer) team. Sport is a weekly thing for me, and I recognize it as essential for my well-being. My nickname playing hockey at university was Rev. In one hockey team I was part of, they used WhatsApp to communicate. Guys getting on a private chat together in a testosterone-filled environment can lead to conversation that's a little rude and crude. I was told that my being on the WhatsApp group cleaned up the chat. I didn't say anything or do anything. I was just there, and people stopped sharing inappropriate material because they knew I was a Christian.

We effect change in and around us by abiding in the One from whom this Kingdom flows, by being yoked to Jesus. As we abide in the vine, its transforming power works in us, producing the fruit of the Kingdom. We had a young guy, a student, coming to our church a few years ago. He came because his pretty flatmate told him he should come. He did, and he stayed. Over the months, I saw a great change in him. He went from listening to worshiping. He started to see himself and the world differently. He found more confidence, joined the worship team, started dating a member of the church, and got baptized. Then he rejected an offer for a good place at a prestigious university, which at the time seemed strange. Eventually he married the girl he was dating and got a great job in the industry that he always wanted to work in—the very job he had wanted to go to university to work towards. He became bold, courageous, and faith-filled. So much change in three years, all because of his growing faith and his rootedness in community. I'm not saying in the vein of the prosperity gospel, "Follow Jesus and all your problems will go and you will become successful and rich." This guy's story continues with highs and lows, but I do want to say that if you follow God, you will grow as a person. It will change you for the better, forever.

When we abide in Jesus and live in relationship with Him, we become a means by which other seeds of His Kingdom spread, affecting the world around us. As a person follows Christ and walks with Him, putting into practice an active and living faith, their attitudes change, their situation changes, and they impact their environments. I believe we can expect to see fruit working itself out in our lives: peace, love, and even joy in the midst of trials and storms. This fruit comes from our planting in Christ, who is seated at the right hand of God. That is the source from which we operate. It is not about white-knuckling it and faking it or putting on a smile when there's something else going on within us. We will need courage, perseverance, and faith, but we can abide in Christ, ground ourselves in God, and be attuned to His voice. It can sound all grandiose, but it is grounded in the daily, in the average of the everyday; from small beginnings comes the greatest things. The smallest seed . . .

Breathe.

Say, "I follow the Prince of Peace."
Listen for Him.
Are you planted in Christ?

CAN YOU HEAR
HIS VOICE?

My sheep listen to my voice;
I know them, and they follow me.

JOHN 10:27

As a parent, I learnt new skills the hard way—through trial, error, and the grind. I quickly learnt my children's cries: a hungry cry, a sad cry, a hurt cry, a "Quick! Something is really wrong!" cry. They all had subtle differences that are hard to describe. I just learnt them—and quick. I also was able to pick out my baby's cry in a room of crying babies. Again, it's not like I could describe why her cry was different. A cry is a cry, but somehow my nervous system, on hearing my kid's cry, knew *That one's mine.* My wife would often talk about "phantom cries." What she means is when you're trying to get to sleep as a parent of a young child, you're so tired that sleep should come easily—but your brain can trick you and make you think you hear crying, so you take the monitor and place it against your ear. But in fact there is no crying or sound—it's just you.

While crying is the way babies often communicate with their parents, gibbons have their own unique way of communicating with each other. When mating, gibbons sing, and when a potential partner sings with them, if their melodies align and sync, they pair. Their song eventually becomes one soulful tune that they continue to sing for life. If the male goes away, the female will sing the song so the male will know not to venture too far out of earshot. It's sweet and kind of a funny thought. But we too can learn the Holy Spirit's tune. We can learn to hear God in the midst of all the noise around us.

Jesus said, "My sheep listen to my voice" (John 10:27). The analogy is a simple one: sheep get to know their shepherd's call. The key to knowing Jesus' voice is firstly to know that He is the Good Shepherd. I had a teacher at school who was a bit of a bully. I knew his voice, but it was scary and loud and accusatory. We had to do what he said because if we didn't, we would get in trouble. We follow Jesus not just because we recognize His voice; we follow because we also know He is good. We follow because we know the One directing us loves us, that we are His beloved, that He wants the best for us. Some of us need to be reminded of this. Perhaps you do hear Him, but do you also know that He is good and that He loves you? That you can trust Him, that He won't lead you to harm? He will lead you to wholeness and healing.

When a shepherd moves his sheep, he calls to them or per-haps whistles or makes a sound. The sheep get used to that sound and respond to it. When I read about shepherds in the Bible, I'm reminded of the three years I spent working as a missionary in a very remote area of Tanzania called Kiteto. Kiteto is home to many Maasai. The Maasai are predominantly herdspeople of sheep, goats, and cattle. When moving their flocks, they use a sort of whistle. Their cattle, sheep, and goats move around them within earshot of the whistle. The animals might not be able to see their Maasai shepherd, but they can hear them, and they walk for days in the right direction because they keep within earshot. The herds know that with their shepherd they will be fed, watered, and protected, so they stay near them. Walking with their shepherd provides them with a sense of peace and purpose in what they are doing; they can relax into the journey not worrying about the direction. It's not that the Maasai hold them by a nose ring and lead them every step of the way, but rather that they know they are moving in the right direction when they hear their shepherd's call. If the first thing to following the shepherd is trusting him, the second is of course the practical step of hearing him.

I'm sure if I asked, many of us would say, "I trust Jesus." But the question for us is, Do we hear and know Jesus' voice?

We have talked about being yoked, abiding in Christ, and now hearing His words. Each aspect here is about the ability to traverse the cobbled road of life with purpose and peace.

So how do we hear God? Because, do not be fooled, we need to train and practice. Of course, God can and does occasionally make it blatantly obvious He is speaking. I once heard the audible voice of a heavenly being—God, or at least an angel—tell me that it was going to rain in three days' time. This was at a time of drought and famine while I lived in Tanzania. Three days later, after months of no rain, the skies burst open, and thunderclouds poured down rain. It was amazing and a powerful moment for me in my faith journey, but hearing God in such a way is rare, and it hasn't happened to me since. I'm not entirely sure why it happened. Did God wish me to pray for this event in order for it to happen? Did He simply want to encourage my faith and let me know He was around and involved? Perhaps both? Whatever the case, I prayed for rain, God said it would happen, and it happened. This memory has been a source of great strength for me, as I know it was real, and nothing can take that from me. However, it is rare that God speaks with an audible voice, and perhaps the reason it's so rare is because the main way God communicates is through relationships embedded within a faith community. The way God usually works is through the Holy Spirit guiding us and teaching us and speaking to our spirit through our community and the Scripture we read. To hear God, we need to know God and be open to hearing Him speak into our lives.

In my parish we have recently become more comfortable

with sitting in silence together. We love worshiping God in song, and we have some amazing musicians, but we have also started a midweek evening service where we sit for fifteen minutes in silence and then do a short compline service. *Compline* comes from the same Latin root as the word *complete*, and it is a short prayerful service meant to end the day—in a sense, to "complete" the day. Monks still practice compline every day around the world. The service is simple and scriptural, with long passages like complete psalms and short single verses from the Old and New Testaments. Being comfortable and confident in your scriptural knowledge is a primary way to know God's voice. Developing an ability to be comfortable sitting in silence—with others or on your own—while being surrendered to any action or intention that God might have, opens you up to getting to know God's presence and voice. Of course, some find it hard at the start. That's normal, but over time our church has developed a core group of people across all demographic lines who keep attending the service and get a lot from it.

There is a rich humanity to be found here in silence with yourself and God. We hear about pollution a lot, but I think noise pollution is a huge danger to our souls and we could all do with rediscovering the gift of silence. Moving into a place of interior silence is not about escaping yourself but becoming truly human. We are not androids, and we are not made up of algorithms. We are humans made in the image of God. He calls us to have faith in Him. Faith is unique to us as created beings. Animals don't have or live by faith. They live by instinct, by their desire, their nature: to eat, to kill, to reproduce. To be human is to live by that which is unique to us, to live by faith in the One who created us. To sit in silence with God has no logical basis. It demands faith, and it teaches us what it means to be human and ironically what it means to be fully alive. To be alive does not mean skydiving, visiting Niagara Falls, or going on a safari. These are all good and great things, but what makes us fully alive, fully human, is to acknowledge God through faith and be with Him, to live out our lives in relation to that truth. Peace and security come from knowing who we are, and that comes from knowing God, who teaches us who we are. We are found in Him, where we are loved, and nothing can take us from that love. When we stand on Jesus, we stand on solid ground. That secure place breathes peace and rest into our lives and any situations we may face.

Breathe.

Move into silence.
Be here with Him who knows and loves you.

THE STATE OF YOUR SOUL

You created my inmost being.

PSALM 139:13

When I was discerning my calling, I worked at a church in Corby in the UK. At the time, Corby was a very poor ex-industrial town. My church was a small Anglican congregation called St. Columba's. One Sunday I was helping the priest distribute Communion, and a lady was brought forward on a medical bed. She was a paraplegic. The only movement she had was in her head: she could move her mouth, tongue, and eyes. I was only nineteen or twenty at the time, and I felt very unprepared to minister to this lady. I looked at her nurse as I held the wafer of Christ's body, and she simply motioned for me to give the woman the bread. I put it to her lips. However, the wafer lay there as she tried to bring it with her tongue into her mouth. She was obviously struggling. I felt a rush of fear come over me. I looked into the woman's eyes as she lay there. She was alive and conscious, and I could see she wanted the bread. She was present with me. I then went ahead and pushed the bread into her mouth. She took it and looked at me and then was wheeled away. Although this powerful moment happened twenty years ago, I still remember it clearly. Her body did not work in many ways, but her soul and spirit were very much alive.

The opposite can be true as well: we can have a healthy body but a paralyzed soul. I grew up with dogs from about the age of eleven. My parents once adopted a rescue dog called Tico. He was a lovely blond Labrador. Sadly, he had been abused in his early years, probably kept in a cage, beaten, and starved. We had him for years. But even after many years with us, he was wary of people. He would always stay close to us on walks while our other dog ran off, and whenever we fed him, Tico would consume his meal in two bites as quickly as possible as if it were his last meal and it would be taken away from him. It was sad to see Tico act like this when he didn't need to.

Similarly, people trapped in shame or abuse or perhaps addiction can have their soul enslaved. We can all be bound to varying degrees. In many cases, it may take professional mental health support to break free.

In my work as a priest, I have met many people struggling with addiction. It is possibly one of the greatest struggles any

of us could go through. When I was in my curacy—a training post for priests—I was assigned to a homeless ministry. I
remember one guy who was smart and very talented at playing
the piano. We actually had a Steinway in the church, and he
would play it. But he struggled with alcoholism, which sadly
he couldn't face up to. When he drank, he made compulsive
and bad decisions, alienated people around him, and spiraled.
He wouldn't admit he had a problem, but he would get angry
all of a sudden. You could be having a nice conversation, and
suddenly he would shift and become loud and aggressive. It was
unnerving. You could see his own self-hatred. It was tragic to
watch. No matter what we did, we couldn't seem to help him
break the pattern of drink and self-loathing. I think of him
often because I could easily be in his place: only a few bad calls
away from a downward spiral. Recently, I have been seeing a
clinical psychologist to help me navigate my life in a healthier
way, to process ministry and its demands. I think it is really
healthy for pastors to do this. Often people look upon us as
flawless, Christlike beings, but we are just like the people in
the pews, trying our best to walk with Jesus. This psychologist
has been helping me to see where perhaps I need to challenge
my own impulses and ways of thinking. He has been helping
me to respond to situations, not react to them; it's like choosing to pause and think before leaping. Fight or flight aren't our
only options. When something comes against us, it's good to

pause and mindfully recognize our feelings. When we observe ourselves, we are better able to make the right decisions in any given moment. It is quite an eye-opener when we question our natural assumptions and come to a different place.

Our souls are powerful and deserve time, thought, and respect. We need to tend to our souls.

As humans, we are made up of body, soul, and spirit. We do not *have* a body; we *are* a body. Greek philosophy and the heretical teaching of Gnosticism taught that the body is bad and the spirit is good. It divided the two in an unhelpful way. The idea of our body as simply a shell we inhabit is not very honoring or valuing of our body, especially in light of the complicated dynamics between our physical brain and our emotions. When we read in Paul's letters about the flesh being sinful but the Spirit giving life (see Romans 8 and Galatians 5), it can sound like this kind of physical vs. spiritual separation. But Paul is talking more about the carnal nature within us that can lead to living in a superficial, emotion-driven way, seeking to satisfy our urges and basic physical appetites. This kind of lifestyle can damage us physically too, rather than cultivating the fruit of the Holy Spirit. Looking more closely at Paul and Christian tradition, we see that our bodies are a gift and God cares as much for the physical as He does for the spiritual. It troubles me when we pitch our mental well-being against our bodies as if the two are enemies. That is not a healthy place to come to. In honoring our body, we honor ourselves; in wounding the body, we wound ourselves. Pope John Paul II described the body in this way: "For a Christian, the body's significance is good, inescapable, and central; Christianity itself cannot be understood apart from an appreciation of the body."[1]

Our spirit is not trapped like a caged animal inside our flesh until the moment of death and then released to bliss. Our bodies are inherently good but still part of the fallen creation which Christ is redeeming. We can be excited that in the resurrection we will receive new bodies. We won't be floaty, ghostlike beings but new physical bodies blazing with God's goodness. This will be a great thing to behold: physical beings but not bound by any fallenness. I believe you will be recognizable in your resurrected body. God cares for us, and that extends to our bodies too. What you do with your body matters, and it affects your whole being.

Psalm 139 speaks of the beauty and preciousness of your body:

> For you created my inmost being;
>   you knit me together in my mother's womb.
> I praise you because I am fearfully and wonderfully made;
>   your works are wonderful,

I know that full well.
My frame was not hidden from you
    when I was made in the secret place,
    when I was woven together in the depths of the earth.
Your eyes saw my unformed body;
    all the days ordained for me were written in your book
    before one of them came to be.
PSALM 139:13-16

There is some use in the classification of our "being" into parts as long as you are not too categorical, as there is much overlap between the body, soul, and spirit. It is simply helpful to acknowledge these aspects of self so we can tend to them and make sure we are staying healthy in every area. You might have heard mention of the body, mind, and soul in a secular context. The Bible talks about our body, our soul, and our spirit. Your body is the most obvious of the three. It is your physicality: your head, arms, legs, etc. Your soul is ultimately your character and what goes into the formation of your character. It's like the decision-making process and the decisions themselves. A simple picture I use to describe the soul is that it's both the washing machine and the washing. You put all this stuff into it, it's all mixed about, and then it's taken out. Hopefully what you draw out of it is clean washing, but sometimes you might have a red sock thrown in—possibly an impulsive bad decision you made or an evil action of someone else—and for that cycle everything comes out a little pink. It's your brain and heart together, if you like. You also have a spirit. You are a spiritual being. Your spirit can discern and know things of the spiritual world around you, insight past the known "worldly" realm. This can lead you and help you but also get you into trouble if you start going down the route of mediums and spiritualists. Your spirit is that which God blows into you as a human, giving you life in His image:

> Then the LORD God formed a man from the dust of the ground and breathed into his nostrils the breath of life, and the man became a living being.
>
> GENESIS 2:7

It is your spirit which connects with God's Holy Spirit and affects your whole being if you allow it. Let me ground this in some Scripture:

> Now may the God of peace himself sanctify you completely, and may your whole spirit and soul and body be kept blameless at the coming of our Lord Jesus Christ.
>
> 1 THESSALONIANS 5:23, ESV

I love how Paul says, "sanctify you completely," then lists the whole of you: spirit, soul, and body. Imagine what it would be like to be holy through and through—in your spirit, soul, *and* body.

Another Scripture passage says this:

> For the word of God is living and active, sharper than any two-edged sword, piercing to the division of soul and of spirit, of joints and of marrow, and discerning the thoughts and intentions of the heart.

HEBREWS 4:12, ESV

In Hebrews, the writer is explaining how powerful God's Word is, how it goes to the very depths of your being. The Word is a living thing, a spiritual thing. It connects deeply with you even to the division of your soul and spirit. I think there has to be a degree of accepting mystery here, as I believe the writer is trying to show that the Word has power and depth that is beyond all that we understand. What we can surmise is the "word of God" referenced here applies to Scripture, in the sense that Scripture is alive, as if the words themselves are dipped in God's Spirit. I have certainly experienced this. But it is not limited to only Scripture. I also think the writer is referring to Jesus as the Word made flesh (see John 1), who, by the Holy Spirit, is among us. In the next verse, the writer talks of how nothing is hidden from God's sight, but everything is laid bare. In this regard he seems to be talking about God's presence in the world, seeing and knowing all.

In the Gospel of Luke, when Mary visits Elizabeth during both of their pregnancies, the Holy Spirit leads her in a moment of spontaneous praise known as the Magnificat. It starts with these words: "And Mary said, 'My soul magnifies the Lord, and my spirit rejoices in God my Savior'" (Luke 1:46-47, ESV).

Mary's soul—her being, her character—magnifies the Lord and praises God, her spirit rejoices, and it is within her body that Jesus grows. It is a kind of trinity of praise with her whole being.

Simply put, you are made up of body, soul, and spirit. This is language we can use to help us understand ourselves and how we work.

Each of these elements can be working and healthy, or they can be damaged and not working properly (or at all). They are of course intertwined and affect each other profoundly. They naturally lead to prosperity of self when healthy, but when unhealthy, they can lead to negative consequences. They can also be independent of each other, and one can be alive and well when the other is in a state of decay.

It is possible to cut yourself off from your spirit, living in bondage to carnal desires and not paying attention to movements and proddings of the Holy Spirit. In Luke 9:60, Jesus rather pointedly tells a want-to-be follower who wishes to bury his father before leaving home, "Let the dead bury their own dead." The impression here is, you can be alive but be spiritually dead. You can also make the mistake of using your spirit to seek out spiritual things without God: practices of witchcraft, mediums, tarot cards, and so on. There may be power there—we are, after all, spiritual beings who can tap into the spiritual world which exists—but we are explicitly told not to pursue these things (see Leviticus 19:31). Opening your spirit in these areas is highly dangerous and an affront to God.

Each of these areas—body, soul, and spirit—is continually being formed in some way, either by our beliefs, relationships, or practices. So let us as God's children be active rather than passive with nurturing them.

———————— ✦ ————————

Breathe.

What is the state of your soul?
Are you feeding your spirit?

SPIRITUAL FORMATION

When you fast...

MATTHEW 6:16

There is a primary school opposite our church, and every year students come across to St. Saviour's to learn about church and what Christians believe. Last year I had a class of eight- and nine-year-olds come across. They were studying sacred places and what goes on in them. I love the inquisitive minds of children. They are constantly searching for answers. One little girl asked me, "Why do you pray in church?" I tried to answer by saying that praying is both really easy and really hard. That you can pray anywhere at any time about anything—that all you need to do is think about God and talk to Him. But I told them it can also be really hard because the world is full of distractions, whether it's homework, cartoons, food, or whatever. We find it hard to slow down and focus on God. Church helps us pause and think about God, and being in a building dedicated to God helps us with this, so we find it is a good place to pray. This simple idea of having things in and around us that help us concentrate on God is the reason for spiritual disciplines. We do them because it helps us grow in relationship with Him. They can help us to focus on God and hear the whisper of His love for us, and let that transform us.

The church has long talked about spiritual practice, or spiritual formation, which is the process of putting things into action to better ourselves as human beings. Perhaps a better way of seeing it is to help us become more fully human, more fully alive—all that God wishes us to be. Less controlled and freer. You may say you are free to make decisions, but how free are you when desire is high and self-control is low? You may know something is wrong, but you are overcome by your wants. Free will is different from freedom of choice. Our will can be driven by various things in our past. It can be self-defensive because of some hurt that has happened to us. We might unwittingly be imitating how our parents react to things. Sometimes we might need mental health support to recognize patterns in our behavior or reactions. Our will isn't *completely* free—it is often damaged and compromised—but it can become *more* free. It's like a compass that wants to point north, but sometimes something sets it spinning or pulls it off slightly. "Too fidgety the mind's compass," said R. S. Thomas.[1] But the more we draw close to God, the more we will learn what true north feels like.

Trying to make the right choices and decisions when we carry so much stuff in our lives can be like driving with a misted windshield. How can you tell where to go and choose the right direction when you can hardly see? Jesus uses the simple analogy of having a plank in your own eye (see Matthew 7:3). He uses this image to describe passing judgment on others, as it highlights that we may each seek to do the right thing but we can't see clearly enough to know what that is. Jesus wants us to see clearly, and that only comes through relationship with Him. True freedom looks more like wanting to—and being able to—choose what is right, naturally, easily, and confidently. This process is what it means to be yoked to God, to abide in Him, and to hear Him. To be pulling in the same direction. It is holistic and feeds us, body, soul, and spirit, and it is the call to discipleship, the call to Christian maturity.

The thing is, seeing our will set free to make the right choices to follow Christ daily doesn't just happen. It takes some work, often a lot of work. You don't walk into the gym overweight and come out trim and muscular the same day; it takes effort and time. You start on low weights and move to heavier ones; you start with a 1K run, then move to a 5K. To be honest, I'm not a gym guy, but you get what I mean. It is a hard truth that we often want the fast, the immediate, but the hard work and grind shows our desire to become what we say we want. Taking our desires and our will and seeking to surrender them to Christ is the walk of a lifetime. Spiritual disciplines help us do this. It's like going to a spiritual gym. You will see results eventually—it just takes a little time. This is not works-based salvation; it is working in partnership with the Holy Spirit for sanctification. It is the movement from being saved *by* Jesus to becoming *like* Jesus.

Breathe.

Are you pulling in the same direction as God?
What is your true north?

You are called to look after yourself, all of yourself. Jesus repeats the Levitical command to "love your neighbor as yourself" (Matthew 22:39)—and how can you love and serve those around you if you hate yourself? You are beautiful and valuable and precious. You have at your disposal a body, a soul, and a spirit, each needing and deserving of attention and nourishment. Let's think about how we might do this. First, your body. Love your body—don't abuse it or mock it—eat well, and exercise. But this is not a law—you don't have to watch everything you eat in some idol-worshiping way. I love a burger and pizza, too, but it is good to have a love and concern for how you treat yourself. You are also called to tend to your soul, to seek to cultivate healthy thought patterns through pursuits such as creativity, music, art, laughter, and fun, not to fill it with evil imagery, porn, violence, and abuse. Often we need help on this, as we have been hurt or affected by something we have done or something someone else has done to us. I remember when I was a student about the age of seventeen, another boy shoved a laptop in my face and said, "Hey, watch this." It was a horrible video of a man being killed. I did not realize what it was until I saw the grotesque murder and looked away. It was awful, and to this day I still remember the images and sounds. We each carry things of injury from our own practice, the practice of others, and the world. But our attitude should be one of seeking to care for our soul and the souls of others.

Your spirit, too, needs feeding and respecting. It is such a source of wonder and grace when we tend to our spiritual growth. Spiritual practices include the obvious ones of worship, prayer, and Scripture reading, and you can add to this the disciplines of silence, pilgrimage, and fasting, all of which feed your spirit. If you are a practicing Christian, you probably do a few of these already. Well done! Keep going! And remember, with all of this there is grace. God's grace is amazing and sufficient for all our needs. I'm not trying to give you guilt or a rod for your back. I just want to encourage you to walk in the knowledge and experience of God's love, and I think these practices will help. Right now I want to focus on fasting—that is, the practice of purposefully not eating—which may be the most neglected spiritual practice of our time. Fasting gives you greater self-control, it helps highlight your weaknesses, and it tends to allow you to hear more from your own spirit and God's Holy Spirit speaking to you. Over time, it allows you to pray with greater ease and fluidity, and you will find your body becomes more alive with spiritual discernment. In a way, it's like putting a controlled stress upon yourself and seeing what rises up within you. It can highlight your weaknesses and things you need to work on. You won't immediately find it peaceful. It is a struggle at first—and, to be honest, it's meant to be.

When I worked in Tanzania as a missionary, a volunteer from the UK wanted to start the practice of fasting. She found it really hard, and she had trouble focusing when she was fasting. When she was teaching a computer class, she mistakenly got them to delete some essential computer files, and about eight computers crashed. It was not a great start! After some tears, she got through it, and we managed to rescue the computers. Making the decision to pursue God through spiritual disciplines is not an easy journey. You might become frustrated or tired, and it's possible you will become more aware of the thoughts, frustrations, and desires that lead you. The practice itself has pitfalls: at first it can lead you to spiritual pride, which is ironic, as you do it to grow with God. Think of the Pharisee in Luke 18 who thanks God that he is not like the tax collector, as he fasts twice a week.

So how does fasting benefit us? There are a number of different benefits: in the Desert Fathers' tradition, it was a way to highlight where the devil might have influence over you so you could more accurately aim at defeating him. Fasting was an expected weekly practice for Christians up until the twentieth century. That is interesting to me. It was commonly known that fasting exposes areas in a person's life that perhaps need more work. When you are hungry, issues like anger, lust, jealousy, and greed come closer to the surface and are therefore more easily acknowledged. Fasting helps you pull the blanket off your idols and expose them. Fasting was used like this by the Desert Fathers to prune their lives, allowing their whole person to be dedicated to God.

Fasting helps us dethrone the bodily urges that often drive us, those urges to jump quickly at a situation—like anger at someone who cuts you off on the motorway or envy for a neighbor's car. It causes us to be more discerning of what is going on inside us and slower to react. Fasting also encourages our spirit to swell, as the practice leads us to think about God more. Right now I am writing this in a café in West London, and I am fasting today. Opposite me for a while was a woman with a four-month-old baby who was calling out nonstop. She wasn't crying, more like getting used to making sounds. This baby was loud! Another time I might have felt annoyed, thinking, *I'm trying to work, and this baby is so distracting I can't think straight,* but I found myself looking at the child and finding it funny and sweet that this baby was learning her sounds. I didn't get annoyed but felt bubbles of joy rising up in me. I reflected that my reaction to see the beautiful and funny side had something to do with my fasting today. If this paragraph doesn't make much sense, you can always blame the child!

For the Desert Fathers and every monastic tradition since, fasting has been and is a regular practice. There is a reason they do it, and there is a reason Jesus fasted and said His followers would do it. He said, "When you fast . . ." (Matthew 6:16), giving the impression that fasting was simply expected. Fasting works!

So, can I encourage you to think about taking it on? My own fasting practice is not to eat food for breakfast and lunch but to have dinner. I usually end the fast around 5:30 p.m. I try to let God lead in how often I do this. My practice alternates between weekly—which I was doing for a year up until recently—to monthly. It is actually written into my rule of life as a third-order Franciscan to fast on the seventh of each month. Remember, abstinence is not fasting. Fasting has to do with food, and food alone. It is a specific spiritual practice.

Stopping social media, while good and worthwhile, is a practice of abstinence, not fasting. Being selective of your diet can be good, but—again it is not fasting. Think of the "Daniel Fast," which is based around the biblical character of Daniel and his friends. When they were taken to Babylon, they refused to eat the food from the king's table, but rather decided to obey God's laws about clean and unclean foods. The Daniel Fast is a strict vegan diet that prohibits animal products, leavened breads, processed foods, caffeine, and alcohol for ten to twenty-one days. For Daniel and his friends, this was not about fasting; it was about choosing not to defile themselves with the king's food and drink. Fasting is a term reserved for stopping all consumption of food for a specified time. You may allow yourself water, of course, or tea perhaps, but fasting always means abstaining from food. Other versions of fasting last an entire twenty-four hours, from one evening to the next. How you do it is up to you. Fasting is hard at first, but believe me, it gets easier and can become part of a weekly devotional practice that leads to great fruit in your life. The practice of fasting has been relevant in every century and every culture, but perhaps even more so now. In the world today where we are so connected and so distracted, to stop and choose self-denial is more appropriate than it's ever been.

I want to include a disclaimer here: for various medical reasons, not everyone should fast. For example, disordered eating can cause great trouble, and if you're at risk, you should probably avoid fasting. When my wife, Jenny, was pregnant, she was very sick and couldn't eat at all. Her relationship with food was complicated for a while, and it would not have been healthy or right for her to fast. We have to be wise with it. God is not a schoolteacher with cane and clipboard monitoring your behavior; He sees and knows each of us and our individual lives. He understands our struggles. If it's safe for you to fast, think about it; if it is problematic for your mental or physical well-being, don't do it. You are loved either way.

Our modern era often celebrates excess. The term *foodie* exists now in our society, and it's not necessarily bad to seek out the best restaurants and celebrate the delicious dishes that creative chefs can muster up. We all like good food, and we are called to be creative. But I think we also need to be cautious, to be self-aware. The ancient Greeks would say, "Nothing in excess," and the Stoics would say, "Everything in moderation." There was a recognition that too much of anything leads to danger. Today, Instagram and other platforms showcase people's belongings, from small things like their trainer collection to larger-scale things like their cars, yacht, or private jet. We celebrate excess, but fasting is about self-denial. In a world where the refrain is "You do you" and "The more the better," the Christian teaching has always been "Deny yourself." This is not for some morbid reason, but for the health of your body, soul, and spirit—and in recognition that if you simply follow every desire you have, you will sooner or later fall to it and hurt yourself and others. So training yourself to deny yourself helps you. You learn to watch your actions, put others first, and not be led by the primal desires that hit all of us. Self-denial is not easy, but fasting helps you build up strength. Remember, our loving Father teaches us that this practice is good for us not because He is a drill sergeant berating us, but because He knows that in this world we will have trouble, and this practice will help us. On school days, we put a snack in our daughter's bag when she has an after-school club, as it will give her a boost of energy for the activity when perhaps her tank is low towards the end of the day. Think of a fasting practice as God's boost of spiritual energy to help us get through life because He wants us better prepared for what might come our way.

There are many passages in Scripture which I could quote regarding fasting and its purposes, but one that stands out for me is from Psalm 4. I consider fasting to be one of the "sacrifices of the righteous" this psalm talks about. It gives a blueprint of why and what happens when we offer this small sacrifice.

Answer me when I call to you,
    my righteous God.
Give me relief from my distress;
    have mercy on me and hear my prayer.

How long will you people turn my glory into shame?

>How long will you love delusions and seek false gods?

Know that the LORD has set apart his faithful servant

>>for himself;

>the LORD hears when I call to him.

Tremble and do not sin;

>when you are on your beds,

>search your hearts and be silent.

Offer the sacrifices of the righteous

>and trust in the LORD.

PSALM 4:1-5

In these few verses, I see a template given. We fast to hear God, we fast to petition for relief and mercy, we fast to expose and destroy false gods (also known as idols), we fast to show our love and devotion to God, and we fast to keep from sinning.

As we put fasting and other spiritual practices into place—recognizing ourselves as body, soul, and spirit and tending to each part, which in turn affects all others—we can abide more with Jesus, walking with Him, carrying His yoke, and hearing Him speak. We will be less rushed and more present. We will hold a greater calm and stillness, which will allow us to walk this life with greater peace and purpose.

Silence the siren voices . . .

Hold back the driving beat of our hearts
and let the drums of our internal wars fall silent . . .

Slow us down for the fast.[2]

———————— ✠ ————————

Breathe.

Where do you need to slow down?
Don't worry; all will be good.

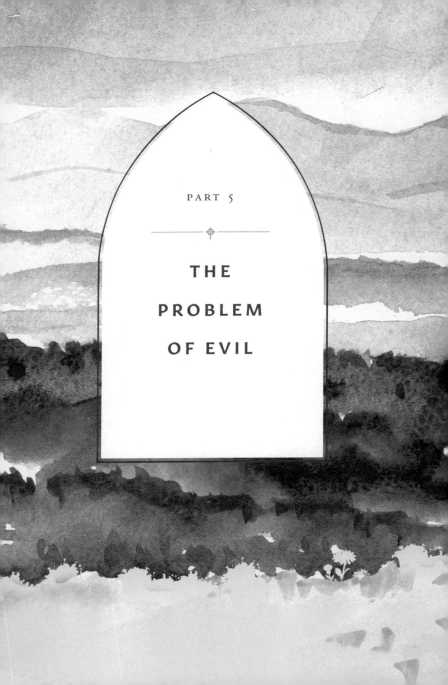

PART 5

THE

PROBLEM

OF EVIL

THE LIES

Did God really say...?

Evil exists, in many forms, in many ways, across continents and cultures—from small, everyday occurrences like gossip and harsh words to big movements like governmental decisions and policies. It seems that the enemy gets a foothold when we don't know and live in the truth that we are beloved of God. I believe the purpose of Scripture is to teach us about who God is and who we are. The great revelation of Jesus was to show us the extent of God's love for us and bring us to an everlasting relationship with Him. It would therefore make sense that the purpose of the devil is to drive us away from God, to stop and limit any relationship with Him, and to cause us harm. In a way, hurting us is a way to hurt God, as He loves us so. Simply put, God wants us to know we are loved. The devil does not want us to know God at all, but if he can't do that, he will try to keep us from knowing that we are loved by God.

As children, we have a simple and clear concept of right and wrong, of good and evil. I might come into the room when my girls are watching a film and say, "What's going on?" They will say something like "These guys are the goodies, and he is the baddie." Film has often tried to associate certain physical attributes with good guys and bad guys. Witches are ugly and have warts; goblins and ghouls look deformed and scary. The Lord of the Rings series features big, loud orcs who are bad, while the elves are elegant and beautiful. In Star Wars, the color of a person's lightsaber is an indication of their character. As soon as a lightsaber turns on, you know something about the person holding it.

The truth is, evil is not always so easy to spot. Recently my wife was talking to a friend whose child has a disability, and she reflected how society and film have often portrayed the evil character with some physical flaw and how that is damaging and sad for people with disabilities. Life is more complex than the movies. That said, there have been times in my life when I have experienced obvious evil, and we shouldn't be afraid to call evil evil!

One day at the mission house in bushland Tanzania, I was relaxing and watching a DVD with some of the students when Danny, a guy who worked for the mission, came in. His brother had been injured, perhaps in a fight, and Danny asked me to bring his brother to a nearby hospital. I took Danny, a couple of students, and a mission volunteer for the journey. As we approached the destination, we asked a few people where Danny's brother was. They pointed us in the right direction. That's when I caught a glimpse of a group of three or four people standing around, and there on the ground with a sheet over him was Danny's brother. I jumped out of my car, and my heart started to thump hard out of my chest. I pulled back the sheet, and what I saw was a bloody mess. He was alive, but his body had been slashed with a machete. It was horrifying. His shoulder was slashed down to the bone, and there were deep gashes all down his back, arms, legs, and head. It seems that the attackers had knocked him to the ground, and then as he lay there, they went to work on him with their machetes, hacking and slashing. It was grotesque violence of a kind I had never seen. We heard that three Maasai had been grazing their cattle on his land, and he confronted them. In response, they had beaten him up and slashed him all over. We quickly lifted him into the car and raced as fast as we could towards the hospital. He made a recovery, but that sort of violence stank of evil.

I have experienced evil in the form of possession and afflictions, and I've been part of a number of exorcisms too. I have witnessed a young girl speaking with a male voice and others coming off the ground in violent convulsions. One teenage boy

I encountered had to be taken out of his confirmation ceremony as the bishop was about to lay hands on him because his body shot up into the air and ran him into the wall of the church. These examples are times when it was clear I was facing evil, but so often the more deadly poison is the one you can't name as poison. So what can we do? Well, there are steps we can take to help us name and navigate evil.

According to Scripture and church tradition, in this life we will face a trifold enemy: the world, the flesh, and the devil. The first thing to notice about evil is that the story of Adam and Eve in Genesis gives us no reason for evil existing: why it is there or where it came from. The story is less about whether evil exists and more about how we are tempted and how we respond to evil. The first thing that happens is the serpent tempts them. He asks, "Did God really say . . . ?" (Genesis 3:1) and suggests, "You will not certainly die" (verse 4). Then they see the fruit looks good and desirable: "When the woman saw that the fruit of the tree was good for food and pleasing to the eye, and also desirable for gaining wisdom, she took some and ate it" (verse 6).

The serpent tempts Adam and Eve, but we are not told why the serpent is there, why the serpent wants to tempt them, or why the serpent himself became God's adversary. We are simply aware that Adam and Eve are given clear and simple instructions, and they break them. The serpent leads them both towards enmity with God. The serpent addresses Eve, but we are also told Adam is with her. Don't forget that! We love to blame Eve, the woman, but we are clearly told, "She also gave some to her husband, *who was with her*, and he ate it" (Genesis 3:6, emphasis added). Interesting to note the action of the man after the Fall is to blame first God and then Eve. "The man said, 'The woman you put here with me—she gave me some fruit from the tree, and I ate it'" (verse 12). *You* put her here, God, and *she* gave it to me! There is a lot of finger-pointing.

What if there and then, instead of trying to justify his action, Adam had simply said, "I'm sorry—I did wrong"?

Here we see the devil, as represented by the snake, leading them through his own corrupted will to come against God. This is a spiritual conflict going on within them. Next we see the example of the world tempting them: the fruit looked good. They were told no, but the fruit was "pleasing to the eye" (Genesis 3:6). They looked and saw that it was good: an external temptation. Then we are told the fruit was desirable because it would lead to gaining wisdom. Desire sprang up within them. This is the flesh. The flesh is linked on an emotional level within our bodies. It is an internal temptation. These three—the world, the flesh, and the devil—are the enemies of every Christian.

You won't die.

God is wrong.

You will become like God if you grab it for yourself.

Do any of those lies sound familiar? When you get confused or are not sure what to believe, make it simple. Ask God to help you replace deceptive thoughts with truth. God is love, and God loves you. You are not perfect, but God is, and He is for you. Yes, evil exists, but so does God—and God is bigger, stronger, and all in for you!

———————————— ⟡ ————————————

Breathe.

What lies are you tempted to believe?
Come back to the truth.
God is on your side.

COME NEAR TO GOD

*Submit yourselves, then, to God. Resist the devil, and he will
flee from you. Come near to God and he will come near to you.*

JAMES 4:7-8

S o how do we understand who the devil is? The red-
horned, pitchfork-holding apparition on our shoulder?
That might not entirely capture who he is.

The Bible is quite clear that the devil exists. The Old
Testament contains only a handful of references to Satan or
the devil. We see the serpent in Genesis. We hear about the
demonic forces in the spiritual realm in books like Daniel
and Job. But it is really in the New Testament that we see a
lot more space given to the devil and demonic activity. Every
time I approach the discussion of evil, I remind myself of the
proper place we as Christians have as victors in Christ. Jesus
has already defeated the devil. Evil won't have the last word in
your life.

To be clear, Jesus was tempted by the devil in the desert following His baptism, and He defeated him then (see Matthew 4:1-11). However, Jesus' ultimate triumph over the devil happened on the cross. The Crucifixion looked like a victory for the power of darkness. In reality, however, the Cross was Christ's victory over Satan. By dying for sinners, Jesus destroyed the devil's claim over us. He took away the devil's power to accuse and condemn. We, too, can have the victory because of God's love, and when we live in this love, we are unstoppable. The devil has no ultimate power over us. As John puts it, "The reason the Son of God appeared was to destroy the devil's work" (1 John 3:8).

When Jesus sends out the twelve disciples on mission, the first thing He gives them is authority over evil spirits. Later He sends out seventy-two people who were part of a large group of followers of Jesus, and again He gives them authority over unclean spirits. When they return from this mission, the first thing they say is "Lord, even the demons submit to us in your name" (Luke 10:17).

Jesus responds, "I saw Satan fall like lightning from heaven. I have given you authority to trample on snakes and scorpions and to overcome all the power of the enemy; nothing will harm you. However, do not rejoice that the spirits submit to you, but rejoice that your names are written in heaven" (Luke 10:18-20).

Jesus gives authority to His disciples and tells them where it comes from: the fact that because their names are written in heaven, they are known and loved. Jesus gives us authority from the same source: our names are recorded in heaven, like a baby-photo book kept by parents. We are God's own. So our position when dealing with and thinking about the devil and the demonic must be rooted in the love of God ultimately shown in the victory of Christ and His defeat of these evil powers.

My wife, Jenny, told me a good story about dealing with evil. When she was a teenager, one of her church youth leaders talked about evil like this: he said that there used to be people whose job was to spot counterfeit banknotes. As part of their training, they would study a real banknote to get used to how it felt and how it crinkled. They would run it through their hands for hours at a time, looking it over, feeling it, even smelling it. Then, when a forged note came into their hands, they would be able to tell because it wasn't quite right. The lesson is that we don't need to get bogged down in studying different types of demonic or occult practices. The better thing to do is to get familiar with God and know His love so that if anything evil comes along, we know it is not from Him.

Once, when I was in university, I was getting a McDonald's lunch. (A vice of mine—don't judge me!) I was in the queue when a lady to my left took my notice. I don't know why, but she grabbed my attention. Something was off. I looked at her more intently: she was wearing a suit, but she had old shoes on. I watched her as she ordered a Coke and sat down. I second-guessed myself and carried on with my lunch. Then I saw her get up and place a bag inside her bag from behind an old lady. She walked out the door, and a guy with a bike followed her.

I immediately rose and went to the old lady. I asked her if she had a bag.

She said, "Yes, it's here," but then upon looking, she noticed it was gone. I ran outside, but the two thieves had disappeared. I felt annoyed with myself. I knew something was wrong, and I didn't stand up immediately when I saw the woman take the bag.

This situation taught me to trust that God speaks, that the Holy Spirit guides us in daily life. That we should firstly be aware of this and secondly be courageous if we sense the Spirit directing us. It gave me an insight into the work of the Holy Spirit. I wasn't sitting in prayer waiting for direction; I was eating a Quarter Pounder with cheese when all of a sudden I was moved. I have a relationship with God, so I should always be aware that He can nudge me anywhere and anytime. My job is to respond.

While this is a negative example, there are positive discernible outcomes to walking in the Spirit, such as being able to discern if someone is called to ministry. Often, I can picture a person in that role. Or sometimes I meet someone for the first time and get the strong sense that they are a Christian. It is not foolproof, but the Holy Spirit speaks. Being confident in Christ is important. The devil seeks to erode our confidence, to try to sow doubt and fear, but we are called to hold to the Rock. If we recognize that the character of God is one of love, and that His love towards us is real and ever-present, then we will surely know that our loving Father wants to communicate to us—and we will have more confidence in listening. Jesus was forever teaching the disciples and those who would listen that the Father loves them, that He runs to them, invites them to banquets, bandages up their wounds, calls them His beloved.

When I think about evil and how we can resist it, I like to remind myself of this story from the Desert Fathers:

> [Abba Elias] also said, "An old man was living in a temple and the demons came to say to him, 'Leave this place which belongs to us,' and the old man said, 'No place belongs to you.' Then they began to scatter his palm leaves about, one by one, and the old man went on gathering them together with perseverance. A little later the devil took his hand and pulled him to the door. When the old man reached the door, he seized the lintel with the other hand crying out, 'Jesus, save

me.' Immediately the devil fled away. Then the old man began to weep. Then the Lord said to him, 'Why are you weeping?' and the old man said, 'Because the devils have dared to seize a man and treat him like this.' The Lord said to him, 'You had been careless. As soon as you turned to me again, you see I was beside you.' I say this, because it is necessary to take great pains, and anyone who does not do so, cannot come to his God. For he himself was crucified for our sake."[1]

Notice in the story, that while the monk felt alone and under attack, the truth was Jesus was always present and ready to save. Often we feel isolated, alone, and far from God, when the truth is He is always with us, calm and ever watchful over us. He asks us only to know and believe this.

I find reading the Desert Fathers very helpful when confronted with the reality of evil. The desert was not a nice place to go on retreat but rather a battleground in which these amazing Christians faced demonic powers and overcame. There are hundreds of stories about demons, and much of the church's understanding of evil is built on the wisdom formed in the desert.

The Fathers were well aware of the intimate union between the body, soul, and spirit—and the war that is waged upon them. They were not just exorcists; they were also, perhaps more profoundly, the first therapists. They would give out advice and prescribe practices to battle the various challenges that afflict a person's soul. They developed lists of teachings under such titles as "On Lust," "On Jealousy," "On Obedience," and "On Self-Control." One famous Desert Father, Evagrius Ponticus, spoke a lot about knowing the enemy's tactics for snaring a monk. His teachings centered on being aware of your thoughts and where they lead you, a practice that is similar to those used today in CBT (cognitive behavioral therapy). He taught that to understand the demonic, the monk must understand and observe his own thoughts. He taught that it was being aware of the thoughts one has that reveals the devil's lies and thus how to counter and defeat them. The Fathers developed a name for this teaching called "guarding the heart."

It is worth saying that while I do believe in the demonic and its ability to affect us and come against us, not every negative thought is caused by a demon. Our worldview should not be one where we see the devil everywhere or blame mental health struggles on demons. My wife once had a very painful prayer ministry experience where she opened up about some specific mental health symptoms she was going through, and the woman praying for her tried to lead her in a prayer of "repentance for partnering with a spirit of hopelessness." We have to be so careful not to call mental health struggles "sin" or "faithlessness" and heap guilt onto people. But we are also spiritual beings, and there can be overlap between our mental and spiritual conditions. Doing CBT or seeing a counselor can be hugely effective for people's mental health. Likewise, spiritual practices can help people find peace and strength as they go through life.

The apostle Paul wrote to the Corinthian church, "We take captive every thought to make it obedient to Christ" (2 Corinthians 10:5). There is something very freeing in seeing dark thoughts that come into our mind as "dark," in acknowledging them as something we experience or contend with rather than as an intrinsic part of ourselves. We are created good by God, but we all contend with darkness and evil.

Evagrius identified eight "afflictions," meaning enemies of the soul. These are common internal thoughts which can take root and lead us to sin and death if we let them. The eight afflictions are greed of stomach, greed of wealth, lust, dejection or sadness (meaning a turning inwards, pulling downwards towards loss and hopelessness, losing touch with reality), anger, sloth, vanity, and pride. Something that Evagrius and the Fathers believed gave rise to these afflictions was the imagination. What he meant by "imagination" was the playground of thought in the human mind—an unquestioned and unrestricted place where thoughts could form, take root, and cause emotions and feelings that eventually lead to action. Now of course the imagination is a wonderful gift to us as humans, but he argued that if not approached with wisdom and discernment but rather left uncontrolled, it could be destructive. Think of how a fire in a pit can provide light and heat and be used as a great tool, but it can also become a thing that burns and destroys if left to its own leisure. The Fathers knew our thoughts could be controlled by primal and fallen forces and our own broken nature. Basically, they would be invaded by the world, the flesh, and the devil.

Now, none of us have total control over our thoughts. They come and go like the wind. We are humans, not robots, but we are capable of questioning our thoughts. We will always experience a cacophony of sensations and thoughts. The question is, What do we do with them? A phrase attributed to Martin Luther says, "You cannot prevent the birds from flying in the air over your head, but you can prevent them from building a nest in your hair."

The Fathers were practical, not just theoretical, which is one of the reasons I think their teaching is crucial for today. Evagrius was a tactician. His gift of teaching was to help the Christian know what's coming at them, how to recognize the enemy, and then how to choose the appropriate weapon against each vice and defeat it. The Fathers believed that a person was to be discerning and learn about the thoughts and emotions that overcame them so they could be better equipped to deal with them. Evagrius said, "Take care of yourself, be the gate-keeper to your heart and don't let any thought enter without questioning it."[2] The Fathers also taught that you could fight the onslaughts of negative thoughts and develop practices that would stave them off. They knew that things like offering hospitality, being generous with people, and inviting them to be with you helped to better the state of your mind and your soul. The Fathers also recommended being sober and practicing meditation. One of the fundamental teachings of the Desert Fathers was living a nonjudgmental life. Their teachings held a lot on the subject of non-judgment. It is interesting that one of the devil's names is the Accuser, the one who seeks to accuse us: "For the accuser of our brothers and sisters, who accuses them before our God day and night, has been hurled down" (Revelation 12:10).

A major attribute of the devil is his propensity to accuse us. The Desert Fathers were very aware that to stand in judgment of anyone is to put yourself in the place of God, and that was what the devil had tried to do. When we judge, we are like the devil seeking to take the place of God, who is the only true judge. We never know the whole story; only God does. Of course we need a legal system and laws in our society. God is a God of order. But the way these systems are set up with trials and juries shows that we don't always know the truth and we should be cautious about passing judgment. While the devil is the Accuser, the Holy Spirit is called the Advocate. The Spirit's role is to help, to teach, to guide, and to defend us:

I will ask the Father, and he will give you another
advocate to help you and be with you forever.

JOHN 14:16

The Advocate, the Holy Spirit, whom the Father will
send in my name, will teach you all things and will
remind you of everything I have said to you.

JOHN 14:26

My dear children, I write this to you so that you will
not sin. But if anybody does sin, we have an advocate
with the Father—Jesus Christ, the Righteous One.

1 JOHN 2:1

A story from the Desert Fathers warning against judging
others goes like this:

One day Abba Isaac went to a monastery. He saw a
brother committing a sin and he condemned him.
When he returned to the desert, an angel of the Lord
came and stood in front of the door of his cell, and
said, "I will not let you enter." But he persisted saying,
"What is the matter?" and the angel replied, "God has
sent me to ask you where you want to throw the guilty
brother whom you have condemned." Immediately he

repented and said, "I have sinned, forgive me." Then
the angel said, "Get up, God has forgiven you. But
from now on, be careful not to judge someone before
God has done so."[3]

Another story I love is about Moses the Black, a wonderful
and wise teacher of the desert. Tradition has it that he was a
reformed thief who repented, found God, and devoted his life
to serving Him. In this story, he is called to a council to pro-
nounce judgment upon a brother who had fallen into sin.

A brother at Scetis committed a fault. A council was
called to which Abba Moses was invited, but he refused
to go to it. Then the priest sent someone to say to him,
"Come, for everyone is waiting for you." So he got up
and went. He took a leaking jug, filled it with water,
and carried it with him. The others came out to meet
him and said to him, "What is this, Father?" The old
man said to them, "My sins run out behind me, and I
do not see them, and today I am coming to judge the
errors of another." When they heard that, they said no
more to the brother but forgave him.[4]

The point is we need to be careful not to set ourselves up
as the bouncers at heaven's gate, making constant judgments of

people and acting as though we're the ones who allow or refuse entry into heaven. It saddens me to see so many preachers at the pulpit condemning the world and other Christians rather than teaching their people about abiding in Jesus and loving those whom they may disagree with. As Jesus so pointedly put it, "Love your enemies and pray for those who persecute you" (Matthew 5:44). St. Francis of Assisi lived in a time when much criticism was directed towards the Catholic church and its rich bishops, arrogant clergy, and monasteries where undisciplined monks ate and drank much better than people in the villages. He taught and showed his brothers a better way rather than standing in judgment. Instead of finger-pointing, he let his actions illustrate the failings of the church. This method revolutionized the church. Richard Rohr, a Franciscan with a great mind, wrote this: "The point of the Christian life is not to distinguish oneself from the ungodly, but to stand in radical solidarity with everyone and everything else."⁵

The disciple Peter (or Simon Peter) was well aware of the devil's schemes, as he had fallen victim to them. The devil effectively tempted Peter to reject Jesus, even though Jesus warned Peter that this would take place: "Simon, Simon, Satan has asked to sift all of you as wheat. But I have prayed for you, Simon, that your faith may not fail. And when you have turned back, strengthen your brothers" (Luke 22:31-32). You may know the story of Peter's denial, recorded in Luke 22.

On this occasion, Peter failed, but, as Jesus prayed he would, he turned back to Him and he strengthened the brothers—including us today. One thing that Peter teaches in his letter 1 Peter is "be alert and of sober mind. Your enemy the devil prowls around like a roaring lion looking for someone to devour" (5:8). I wonder if Peter had in mind his own falling when writing such words to strengthen the church.

Let us be aware of the devil—Satan, the Accuser—and the demonic world around us without being fearful but being confident in Christ. Let us learn the wisdom of the church and its teachers, being humble and discerning of thought, practicing hospitality and sobriety, withholding judgment, and seeking God in prayer. As James tells us, "Submit yourselves, then, to God. Resist the devil, and he will flee from you. Come near to God and he will come near to you" (James 4:7-8).

Let's come near to God, being confident in His love and care for us. This book is called *Know You Are Beloved* because I'm trying in every chapter to help us to see our place as first and foremost loved by God. When the Desert Fathers taught tactics to defeat the enemy, these all came from a place of knowledge of God's love for them and God's presence with them. When you have a big brother on the playground, you don't have to worry about the bully in your class. This place of security in the love of God will help us not to fall or point fingers at others. It will lead us to show greater grace towards the failures of others. A modern-day sign that highlights the insecurity of our understanding of God's love for us is the rise of cancel culture. Sometimes I feel like justice is now in the hands of the comments sections online. I find it deeply troubling how quick people are to condemn and judge anyone and everyone for their mistakes, whether large or small. Whenever I'm tempted to jump onto the comments to say my piece, I stop, take a breath, and don't! When did we forget that people make mistakes? They don't need condemnation; they need mercy and forgiveness. Let us rest in the knowledge of God's mercy and love towards us. When we do, we are less likely to condemn others.

A practical tool that will help you to resist evil and walk a healthier faith path is to be part of a loving community. You will be shaped by who you hang out with, either positively or negatively. I have noticed in my own life that the people I spend time with affect how I think, react, and behave. When I was young, studying for my first degree and distant from God, I hung out with a group of guys whose activities were less than wholesome. We would smoke, drink, chase girls, and gamble, and all of this became common and everyday. I felt quite lost, alone, and unhappy. In contrast, when I was studying in Cambridge, living in a theological college among others who were hungry and thirsty for God, I was encouraged and built up. In my second year, I lived with three guys whom I still hang out with and pray with today: John, who was super smart and spoke Greek and Hebrew and German on the side; Greg, a big rugby guy who loved and knew the Bible inside and out; and Callum, a worship leader who loved praising God. I was the prayerful one. We all brought something to the group, and it was one of the greatest years of development for me.

This is one reason for being part of the church community: to be around those who encourage you and love you and whom you can be open and honest with. I know the church is not always like this, but it should be. Having good friends and mentors you can trust with your good and bad stuff will help you keep the world at bay. Practicing healthy hobbies like going to the gym, listening to music, reading, and keeping track of your mental health will help you keep your flesh in check. Hiding away and detaching yourself from other people will not stop you from being tempted and going through trials. Often the isolation makes it worse. A classic warfare strategy is "divide and conquer." Napoleon swore by it as he carved up Europe, and it is no different in the spiritual realm. The devil will try to split you off from community. Remember: "Our struggle is not against flesh and blood, but against the rulers, against the authorities, against the powers of this dark world and against the spiritual forces of evil in the heavenly realms" (Ephesians 6:12).

Praying, worshiping, fasting, going to church, and serving

will all defend you against the devil, as these practices build up your spirit. Like going to the gym to get fit and build up muscle, so, too, you build up your spiritual muscles by practicing these disciplines. Keeping yourself healthy at these levels will give you strength to overcome the world, the flesh, and the devil. This, in turn, will help keep you rooted in the truth that you are loved and found in who God says you are.

———————— ✦ ————————

Breathe.

Remember:
Christ has defeated the devil.
Evil will never win.
Come near to God.

18

JOY!

For the Joy set before him...

HEBREWS 12:2

I have met a few people over the years who carry a powerful fruit of the Spirit, one which you can't help but be sucked in by and which affects you being near it. That characteristic is joy! Joy is often overlooked, perhaps underrated, and at times misunderstood. But joy is a powerful weapon. The One who wields it is the One whom the powers of darkness flee from. It is interesting to me that in the Harry Potter universe, the way to battle the boggart—the evil creature who takes on the form of your greatest fear—is to laugh at it, to see your fear and meet it with laughter. Now I'm not saying I get my theology from Hogwarts, but there is something there. The devil hates to be mocked. I wanted to follow the chapters on evil with a chapter on joy for this very reason. Where there is joy, evil flees.

When evil rises and wishes to see you thrown into fear and chaos, you can stand on the victory of Christ and recognize the power and place of Jesus and the resources that are at your disposal. At these times, you can have joy bubble up inside of you. Joy knows its place of security. It knows the Father's love and His willingness to save, so much so that as Paul declares in Romans 8:38-39—one of the greatest statements in all of Scripture, expressed with great joy—"I am convinced that neither death nor life, neither angels nor demons, neither the present nor the future, nor any powers, neither height nor depth, nor anything else in all creation, will be able to separate us from the love of God that is in Christ Jesus our Lord."

If you need any more convincing of the power of joy, remember the gift that gave Jesus the strength to go to the cross: "For the joy set before him he endured the cross, scorning its shame, and sat down at the right hand of the throne of God" (Hebrews 12:2).

It was joy, the joy that Jesus saw was to come—I think not just for Him, but for us all. Joy was the strength that helped Jesus suffer perhaps the most brutal suffering of anyone, bearing the weight of sin and the pain of being crucified. Joy is powerful!

Having joy is not about the absence of pain or hardship. It is about presence; it is about having something. That something is God. It is having His security, knowing His love, and knowing His presence with you. If I go to the park with my kids, my four-year-old will review the area: *Where will I go?* Some things she will wander to and go on herself, like the slides or the roundabout. But the more challenging things like the monkey bars she won't try alone. She will call me over: "Daddy, come here!" I will go stand with her as she tries to hold on and move her hands between the bars. There is still a level of fear: she doesn't want to slip off. But when I'm there, she also knows, *Daddy will catch me. He is with me.* So she goes for it, and if she does fall, I'll catch her, pull her into myself, and maybe do a kind of bear growl, and she will laugh and giggle and want to try again. Her knowledge of my love and presence gives her security and boldness, and joy comes with that as she knows she can overcome this difficult thing. It is great to see.

I know many Christians who, over time, slowly forget the awesomeness of God. We can become the Prodigal Son's older brother. The one who stayed behind, who was good but who sadly lost sight of his father's love and resources. He needs to be reminded that his father's land, house, and cattle belonged to him, that the Father loved him too. It is easy for us to do the same thing. We forget the magnitude of our faith, the wonderful truth that God has saved us, loves us, and is ever with us. The world around us, with its noise and distraction, moves our sight away from Jesus.

Can I remind you that God is with you? He never left you. When He sees you now, He also sees you in glory, praising Him in the Kingdom to come. This is a wonderful truth, and I pray it helps joy bubble up in you. You are more than a conqueror!

Pause.

Breathe in deeply.
Say, "I am safe. I am loved."
Now smile!

PART 6

HOUSE

OF

PRAYER

DISCOVER DEEP REST

Our heart is restless until it rests in you.

AUGUSTINE, *Confessions*

W e live in such a turbulent world, a world where anxiety, fear, and hopelessness are seemingly always present. Wars, political instability, and division have, in fairness, always been around, but right now these concerns seem more visceral and dangerous than anything I have experienced, certainly in my lifetime. We are recovering from a pandemic, but its impact on us is still present.

When I've talked with people about their lockdown experiences and how they are doing now, it seems we have all been humbled and reminded of our humanity and fragility. We have each had to spend more time with ourselves, whether this looked like being busy at home without our usual support network or literally being alone for long periods of time.

We were confronted with our own minds, perhaps our own weaknesses. It was a hard time for a lot of people. I certainly learnt things about myself and what I rely on to fill me up or calm me down, what structures are helpful. When we were unable to make plans, my family and I had to focus on the present in a way that made us look at how we function day-to-day. Outside of the pandemic, we have things in our hearts and minds that we might never engage with if we're always working towards the weekend, the next holiday, or whatever it might be.

There is a story from the Desert Fathers about three monks who loved to work for God. One went to the nearby town to see where there was strife and try to turn it to peace. The second chose to go about and visit the sick. The third one went to the desert so that he might dwell in quietness. The man who sought to bring peace between men found he could not make every man be at peace with his neighbor, and his spirit was sad. He went to visit the man who sought to be with the sick, but found him to be sad as he could not fulfill the law which he laid down for himself.

Then the two of them went to visit the monk in the desert. Seeing each other, they rejoiced. They asked this monk how he had lived in the desert. He was silent. Then he asked them each to fill a vessel with water, and they did so. He asked them to pour some of the water into a basin and look down into it.

Next he asked them what they saw, and they replied, "We see nothing."

After they had let the water settle, he said, "Look again."

They replied that they saw themselves clearly.

The monk in the desert replied that the troubles of the world are a disturbance that does not allow you to see yourself and your sins, but the one who lives in peace and quiet is able to see God clearly.[1]

Following the pandemic, many people emerged changed. It was an opportunity to walk out into a new world with a new worldview. We got a new look at ourselves and our lives and had the chance to rethink some things. Some have been able to maintain their vulnerability and see deep change. Their water has stilled. Others quickly sought to return to their distractions and slowly regressed. Suffering is a catalyst for change, and the world went through a great suffering in lockdown and through the pandemic. We can use it and learn, or we can run from the vulnerability. In the Bible, ironically, the physical desert has always been a place for fruit to grow in the lives of God's people.

What has grown in your life?

Here in London, there was a mass exodus during and immediately after the pandemic lockdown period. Many people sold up and bought houses in the countryside. Since working from home became an option, people could live outside the city while keeping their jobs. The move from London to the countryside was so prevalent that a number of schools, which in London are usually full with long waiting lists, had spaces open up as families moved away. That's what happened with us, as our eldest daughter, who was initially refused entry to a particular school, managed to get in after a space became available and the school had no one to fill it. House prices in London stalled for a time, as many were selling to move out and the market became buoyant with property. It seems many people were tired of London and its busyness and wanted a greater stillness and peace, and they believed they would find this in the English countryside. I have heard recently that many are looking to move back to London now as they miss the big city. Stillness and peace are the result of an attitude change more than a geographical one.

We long for rest, a deep rest in our souls.

We have a sense that it is possible. We taste it now and again, tap into it in moments of love, acceptance, and beauty. We can experience it with friends and loved ones in those great moments of laughter and abandon. We know it exists, but it eludes us so often. Like a dog chasing its tail, we know it's there, but we can't grasp it. The fact that we know it's real but out of reach only adds to our anxiety. The rise of mindfulness and the teachings around "being present" are helpful. But, as Augustine famously said in his *Confessions*, "Our heart is restless until it rests in you."[2] It is to God that we must turn. It is in prayer and communion with God that this rest can be found and retained, not only bumped into but kept. It is not just okay to rest in God; it is crucial and holy. As Psalm 23 describes it,

> He makes me lie down in green pastures,
> he leads me beside quiet waters,
> he refreshes my soul.

PSALM 23:2-3

———————— ✢ ————————

I believe that all of us are built for prayer. It is funny to me that prayer is both natural and kind of strange. I remember praying from a very young age and mostly accepting the simple truth of it: that when I direct my thoughts towards God, He hears them. The intention led the direction. I remember when I finished praying, I would cup my hands together and blow through them as if I were blowing my prayers up to God. The concept of prayer didn't need a lot of explaining. Did it?

If you were to stop a hundred people on the street and ask, "Have you ever said a prayer?" all of them—without exception, I would guess—would say yes. Whether it's before an exam, at a birth, to give thanks, or when we experience loss or grief, prayer

comes naturally to us. There is something within us that points
to a greater reality around us and seeks it. Like gravity, the Holy
Spirit draws us. However, while prayer is natural, continuing
in it is also grossly difficult. Do you recognize that? Have you
noticed that it's easy to go to the gym occasionally, but it's difficult to be consistent? That is certainly my experience! A hard
truth is that to be persistent in good works takes huge effort,
while sinning is easy. One takes effort to keep on going; the
other just happens effortlessly. Here is a Desert Fathers story
I read on prayer that encourages me:

> The brethren also asked [Abba Agathon], "Amongst
> all good works, which is the virtue which requires the
> greatest effort?" He answered, "Forgive me, but I think
> there is no labour greater than that of prayer to God.
> For every time a man wants to pray, his enemies, the
> demons, want to prevent him, for they know that it is
> only by turning him from prayer that they can hinder
> his journey. Whatever good work a man undertakes,
> if he perseveres in it, he will attain rest. But prayer is
> warfare to the last breath."[3]

The world is a loud, turbulent place, and often the same
is true of our interior selves. We are distracted and anxious.
Our attention is fleeting; we often give it to everything except

prayer. Prayer is wonderfully powerful, and because of that, the world, the flesh, and the devil all gang up to keep us from it—whether through external occurrences or an internal battle in the heart or mind. William Butler Yeats, who received the 1923 Nobel Prize in Literature, elegantly describes the problem of the mind in his poem "The Balloon of the Mind":

Hands, do what you're bid:
Bring the balloon of the mind
That bellies and drags in the wind
Into its narrow shed.[4]

As a balloon on a string in the wind moves this way and that even in the lightest breeze, so our minds are easily distracted and shoot around. The hands in this poem are the means by which we can seek to bring our mind to stillness and control.

Another great writer, Charlotte Brontë, wrote, "A ruffled mind makes a restless pillow."[5] How often we feel tired, but as soon as we get to our pillow, off races our mind. It is like the pillow is the starting gun for a race.

Our solution lies in God. To come back to the place of love and security. Don't try to force the other thoughts out, but move your thought to God, to His love, and to truth. Picture it as a screen swipe on your phone: swipe up to higher thoughts, swipe up to God.

While we experience great difficulty stopping, concentrating, and giving our attention to one thing, God does not. While we find it hard to be present in the moment, God is able to give His whole attention to all things and to each one of us simultaneously. Throughout Scripture, we read about God's attentiveness to us. For example, in Matthew 10:29 Jesus says, "Are not two sparrows sold for a penny? Yet not one of them will fall to the ground outside your Father's care." Psalm 139 describes our inability to escape from God.

> You know when I sit and when I rise;
>> you perceive my thoughts from afar.
> You discern my going out and my lying down;
>> you are familiar with all my ways.
> Before a word is on my tongue
>> you, LORD, know it completely.
>
> PSALM 139:2-4

We are known completely by God. We are the apple of His eye (see Psalm 17:8), and His gaze is never off of us. It is as we sit in His gaze that we can simply look back to Him and find that we have arrived at true stillness. Prayer is not about trying to fill your mind with God to force the other stuff out. Rather, it is an honest position, held before the One who knows us honestly. Rest in the arms of the One who loves you.

You can discover a deep rest in God.

Breathe.

Rest.

SURRENDER

By waiting and by calm you shall be saved.

ISAIAH 30:15, NAB

For me, one of the most profound Scripture verses on prayer is from Exodus 14:14: "The LORD will fight for you; you need only to be still." It reminds me that prayer is a decision to stop and trust, to accept that all prayer is surrender: ultimate surrender of self to God. I love the simplicity and the profoundness of the passage. It's just saying,

Stop.

Be still.

Let go,

Let God.

It is that simple.

Let go of your endless pursuit for control.

Let go of trying to figure out your own way.

Let go of it all.

Just know God.

Know that God is always going to be God. He will always be in total control. He possesses absolute sovereignty. The key teaching of Christ is important here: God is your Father who knows and loves you.

So be still and know Him.

I love what St. Francis says about the way Franciscans are to pray:

> Wherever we are we carry with us our cell, for Brother body is our cell and the soul the hermit that dwells therein, praying to God and meditating on Him. If the soul cannot keep quiet and recollected in her cell, there is little use for a cell built by hands.[1]

We are then—each of us—a house of prayer, called to be a people of prayer. We shouldn't allow our souls to be overrun and have our peace stolen by the world and our desires. As the book of Isaiah says, "By waiting and by calm you shall be saved, in quiet and in trust shall be your strength" (30:15, NAB).

I love to pray, and I recognize a difference in myself if I go for some time without praying. My soul becomes restless. I answer people and problems out of a rushed place. In order to satisfy my desires, I turn to quick stimulation like picking up my phone or turning on Netflix. I rush more. I, like you, am a pilgrim on the cobbled road of life trying to navigate it as best I can. And I just know prayer helps. It helps a lot! But in a busy life, often the first thing to go is prayer time.

When I was at theological college training to be a priest, at the end of the year we would head into the exam term. Everyone and everything seemed to turn towards deadlines, revision techniques, and timetables. It was easy to let your prayer life go in order to get more work done. I was thankful that in this time, my gut response was not to pray less but to pray more. I knew I needed help, I needed God. Of course I revised and got my work in, but I also prayed. In a world of measurement and success, prayer seems to be unmeasurable, so its value in our eyes is diminished. To sit and do nothing but bring thoughts, worries, and hopes to God makes so many of us feel like we are wasting time. I feel it too. There isn't enough time to do everything, but prayer works.

I think so many of us are like Peter at the Mount of Transfiguration when he witnessed Jesus transformed and saw Moses and Elijah next to Him. Luke records that Peter said they should make tents to honor the moment. But then

Scripture says that Peter did not know what he was saying (see Luke 9:28-33). I find that Bible passage funny. Peter was thinking like we often do: *I must do something. I must mark this moment.* But then God came in a cloud, rested over them, and told them to *listen* to His Son (see verse 35). God was essentially saying, "Just be quiet, Peter. Stop trying to do. One thing is required: listen to My Son, Jesus."

My wife, Jenny, and I had a profound encounter once. We were staying at my parents' house, where I grew up. We were both asleep one night when we were suddenly woken up. I don't know how to explain it, but we were woken up by and into God's presence. I remember uttering Jenny's name, and she simply said, "I know." We were both aware of God's amazing presence around us. I responded by saying, "Wow!" and giggling. Jenny, next to me, was just as amazed by all of it. We held hands and shared that awesome moment. But instead of just staying in the moment and being present with God and each other, after a couple of minutes, I began to think that God must be wanting something from me: perhaps I should get up and pray around the house. I leapt into action: I got up, walked around the house, and prayed. If I could go back, I would have calmed down my past self and encouraged him to simply stay in bed, next to Jenny, enjoying God's presence. I look back at myself with utter frustration. How could I have squandered that moment with my senseless activity? We, as members of the Kingdom of God, are called to be countercultural: we are called to stop, pray, and trust the invisible God who is at odds with the world's ceaseless mantra of *do*. We are quick to rush and worry, but God is surrounding us. Think of the story from 2 Kings when an army surrounds Elisha to kill him. His servant is terrified, but Elisha is calm: "'Don't be afraid,' the prophet answered. 'Those who are with us are more than those who are with them.' And Elisha prayed, 'Open his eyes, LORD, so that he may see.' Then the LORD opened the servant's eyes, and he looked and saw the hills full of horses and chariots of fire all around Elisha" (2 Kings 6:16-17). If we were to for a moment see how present God is, how He loves us, I think we would spend a lot less time anxious and rushed.

Surrendering to God and being in His presence is not about setting aside hours every day. If you can, great, but we are not all monks living in monasteries. It is more about taking moments to stop and punctuate your day with prayer. Build in a daily quiet time, perhaps try to start and end your day with five to ten minutes of prayer. Sit, breathe, welcome God, pray, and read your Bible. Along with this, develop an attitude of prayerfulness that inhabits your daily life. We want prayer to be close to us, an easy option for us.

I'm always amazed by people who can speak multiple

languages. We have a woman in our church who is Korean Canadian and speaks four or five languages. A family from France visited our church while on holiday. I asked if she could speak to them, and with gentle ease she moved from speaking with me in a Canadian English accent to perfect French in a French accent, her Canadian tones gone. The French family's eyes lit up as they understood her, and they talked back and forth. If we can keep prayer close to us and use it regularly, it will become second nature. We will find ourselves praying without thinking. This happened to me the other day. I was visiting my mum and dad and had a great time in our family home. I walked out of their old farmhouse into the front garden area. The sun was warm upon my face, the birds were singing, and the small ponds were bubbling with fish swimming. I just started thanking God for the time there with my family before I knew what I was doing.

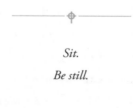

Sit.
Be still.

Breathe.

Find your deep rest in God.

PART 7

GOD

WITH

US

GOD BECAME A BABY

The God of the universe became a wiggling
baby in order to get close to you.

TIMOTHY KELLER

I believe God's hand has always been on me. But while I knew something of Him at a younger age, I did not surrender to God's lordship over my life until I was near twenty. In the past, I have referred to my BC life and AC life, meaning my "Before Christ" and "After Christ" life. I know some people have a "road to Damascus" conversion, where something dramatic happens and they can name the time and the place they started following Jesus. But for most of us, being "born again," like a human birth, takes time and has been growing for a while beforehand. It is not a sudden event but a series of small and incremental happenings that occur over time. Months pass, and we grow slowly. Then more months go by, and we realize, *Actually, yes, I do believe and now live by God's Word.* It is like riding the train through the Channel Tunnel into France from England. I never exactly know what moment I hit the French waters. I'm in a dark tunnel, after all. But I know I'm on my way there, and the key thing is that I arrive in France. Having said that, whatever way each of us comes to know Christ, there is a marked change from our BC life to our AC life. Change often takes time, but it always happens. I have noticed this in others, *and* I have noticed it in myself. The Holy Spirit is always at work. A new relationship with Jesus deepens. A person's perspective on life changes. Where once we lived in and of the world, we now live by a new law—one of grace that produces hope and a new way of seeing. Certainly that is how it was for me. I went from living for myself, for pleasure, and for what gains I could make to suddenly being aware of another world—one where a loving King rules, where a King gave His life for me and helps me to understand my place in it all. I started to see myself and the world in a completely different way. I knew I was loved, as was everyone and all of creation.

Everything changed for me.

I saw something new.

The church has a word for all of this: *conversion.* One definition describes it as "the process of being changed." We are converted from one set of beliefs about ourselves and the world to a new set of beliefs. It is a big deal. Everything can be shaken, and we don't know what it will mean for us. All we know is that we have to keep going.

There's a story about St. Francis which fits well here. One day he was out with brothers on an evangelistic mission when they came to a crossroads. They did not know which way to go. Should they turn left? Or right? Francis told them to start spinning around and around, which they did. Then, with his eyes closed, he shouted, "Stop!" Whichever way they faced, they went.[1] Similarly, we can feel in a spin when we come to God, not knowing what it will mean for us or where He is going to take us. One way to interpret Francis's command is that it didn't matter which way they went as long as they trusted in God. Another is that in the action of spinning, they let go, and God was able to point them. Both conclusions require faith and trust. My own take is to walk in faith in the direction your life is currently going, accept your circumstances, trust God will guide you, listen for His guidance, and expect it. Don't allow fear and worry to stop you from making decisions. You can't steer a parked car—it needs motion—so move and know God is with you.

Simply trust in God.

Go—where you are pointed.

———————— ✦ ————————

I can't name the day I found Christ, but I remember making the first real decision in my life—*for my life*. I was twenty-one with a career in business ahead of me, a house, a mortgage, and family expectations. In the midst of all this, I booked a ticket to Tanzania to work at a small mission. I quit my job, put my house on the market for rent, and told my parents that I was leaving. Inside, I was spinning. It was risky, but I was also taking control by making a decision to go. Clearly, I was searching and looking. Now I see that Christ was calling me at that time. I went to Tanzania and fell in love with Jesus. I came back completely changed. I spent three years moving back and forth between Tanzania and the UK. I would go out for long periods of time, then come back for a few weeks and raise money in the UK, and then go back to Tanzania. I was ordained in the Diocese of Mount Kilimanjaro at the age of twenty-four. I set off in the direction of God, and I haven't stopped pursuing Him since. Obviously, I stumble and trip up on the road, but I have never left the path.

I stepped into the current of God's will for my life, and it changed absolutely everything.

I'm still being changed today, as my conversion to Christ is not a one-off, but more like a rocket heading into space. There was the initial launch, which used a great amount of energy. Then, once the rocket is in space, less dramatic adjustments are needed so everything can stay on course. Those are the small conversions in our lives: the thought patterns that change, the decisions that need adjusting as fresh insight comes, and much more. We are not launched and then left. We are consistently challenged and called into a greater relationship with our Creator.

One thing that never ceases to amaze me is the Incarnation: God with us.

I think the Catholic church has an incarnational attitude that all of us can learn from. Did you know all those paintings of Mary and Jesus that you find in Catholic churches are pointing to one of the greatest and most profound truths of Christianity? God *became* a baby.

In most of these paintings, Mary is looking at Jesus, and Jesus is looking at the viewer. In some paintings, Mary's hand gestures towards her Son, as if she is saying, "Look at Him." The point is to remind the viewer of the Incarnation. God became flesh. He did this for you. Think about what that means for you.

How does this change everything?

How do we live incarnationally? It should draw us *not* to simply see Christ but also to see as Christ sees. There is a wonderful story about St. Francis that grips me whenever I read it. It makes my mind bubble and fizz. Francis had gone up to Mount La Verna, an area of land he and his order had been given by a rich nobleman. He was fasting and praying in the lead-up to Easter. It was here that he had an amazing vision. He looked up and saw a man above him. The man was like a seraphim—an angel which had six wings: two high in order to cover his face, two to fly with, and two to cover his feet. As Francis looked, the winged figure remained a seraph but was also Christ crucified. Imagine Francis looking up and seeing Christ crucified but simultaneously with wings: two straight above his head, to be able to shield his face; two stretched out in flight; and two pointing down to the ground and able to shield his feet. The image represents the divinity of Christ simultaneously with the humanity of Christ. It is a symbol of great pain and burning love held together. It is seen by some commentators as God consuming pain into His divinity and making suffering holy, not just Christ's but ours, too, when we suffer with God. Standing up following the vision, Francis looked at his hands, and there appeared images of the wounds of Christ, which is called the stigmata.[2] St. Francis was the first person to receive such wounds.

Obviously this is hard to grasp, and of course you don't need to believe it, though I do. Some insist that Francis had leprosy, and this story was a way to explain away the sores. In any case, I believe Francis had an incredible vision of Christ that helped him see this world through an eternal lens. We are all called to be an incarnation of the Incarnation. This is no new teaching. We are called to be Christlike in the world: to be Christ's presence in our families, our workplaces, and wherever else we find ourselves. As Paul writes in Romans 13:14, "Rather, clothe yourselves with the Lord Jesus Christ." This is not easy, though, and we will each struggle in our own way to live like Jesus. More often than not we get it wrong. When we do, we see that the undeniable work of grace in our lives is the real transforming factor bringing us into deeper revelation of who Jesus is.

Breathe.

God is present—with you.
Clothe yourself with Christ.

A BEAUTIFUL MESS

Lord, who are you? And who am I?

ST. FRANCIS OF ASSISI

I love my children. They are my life—the wealth of my life. Of course they do naughty things, and I can usually tell when they are up to mischief simply by looking at them. But I love their whole being. I can hold and consume their failings in my love, and if needed, I would lay my life down for them. I want them to know they are loved, and I want them to experience my love. Knowing that they do gives me the greatest joy. In my work as a priest, I have been around dying people and sat with them in their final moments. The words they utter to their family if they are able to—and the words of the people around them—are always the same: "I love you." Why? Because knowing we are loved is the point of life. It's ground zero of everything.

God wants you to know that you are loved. The Incarnation shows us that, and having a good understanding of the Incarnation will help you understand that you are loved. God became flesh to be with us. He loved, laughed, wept—and He was also beaten and killed for each one of us. The great patterns of God's love are revealed in our world. He loves and cares for us. How do we know that? Love is action, and our God is a God who came towards us. His action teaches us who He is and who we are.

God draws near.

Living in the light of the Incarnation is much deeper than simply trying to do the right thing or having the right answers. It is about accepting who we are, as revealed by Jesus Christ. He is "the firstborn over all creation" (Colossians 1:15), not the only born. We were created by God, we fell, and then we were redeemed by God through Christ and restored to our place as God's children following in the footsteps of Jesus, the firstborn. We join Christ as children of the Kingdom. In this section of Scripture, Paul is trying to help us see our place as God's beloved and then act accordingly. Jesus ushered in the Kingdom, and we are its residents. We are called to live out this Kingdom residency. As I mentioned in chapter 1, St. Francis had this great prayer: "Teach me who You are. Teach me who I am."

Our own identity is wrapped up in God and also revealed in the Incarnation: the life, death, and resurrection of Jesus.

You are not a mistake. You aren't a chunk of flesh, randomly formed in this time and age. No, you are wonderfully made, with purpose, bearing the image of God within your very being. He knew you would be alive today, in this time, in this culture, so you have everything you need to overcome. Today, as in the early church, we see the rise of many troubling cultural shifts. But perhaps you are here because you are one of God's great warriors whom He positioned for this time. He draws you out; God names you as His. You are called into the eternal truth that you are loved and saved by your Creator. This truth marks your life, and living it out sets your life apart as holy. You become involved in God's Kingdom, redeeming creation.

Yes, suffering and brokenness and pain and rejection will also be part of your experience. Failing—and accepting your failings with repentance—is a greater part of God's call than your success is. It is perhaps the most profound sign of your Kingdom residency.

Through all of it, you are called to know this:

You are loved, and you are to love as Christ loved.

There is a cosmic pattern of death and resurrection working in the largest and the smallest parts of our lives, and through it all God is drawing us ever deeper. Great mysteries express themselves in the everyday. They are written into everything, and we are invited to see. That is why the Desert Fathers could take themselves into the depths of the Egyptian desert, away from the world, and still experience the great movements of God. As we grow in our journey with God, we become more like Christ. It happens in our normal relationships: you become more like the people with whom you hang out. Likewise, we move in our conversion from seeing Christ, to being transformed to seeing as Christ sees, to acting as Jesus would act, to loving as He loved. This is incarnational living. It is realizing your connectedness with God, your true place in the Kingdom of Heaven. What the Incarnation also reveals is that we are not saved from our flesh, taken away from the physical or called to somehow leave it behind. We are saved through it. Jesus is a physical being. He has a body and was raised in a body; thus the redemption we get like His is physical too. God loves you, all of you. How could He not? Yes, you are broken and will sin and are called to repent, but this, too, is dealt with on the cross. You are invited in your humanity to share in His divinity—to be like Christ. The model is Jesus, both human and divine. You will carry weaknesses your whole life, and you are called to bear them, acknowledging your weaknesses as well as your beauty.

God sees us through the lens of Christ when we come to Jesus. As the apostle Paul teaches, we are "in Christ"

(Romans 6:11), and God sees us this way. Christ died in pain and suffering, alone, naked, and rejected. The human weakness He bore is not stripped from us, but it was dealt with by Him. You will still sin; you will still get it wrong. You are not perfect. Christ is, though. Let us not fall into thinking that Christ is the only one whose humanity is loved by God and we are *only* loved by God so far as we are Christlike. God loves each one of us and delights in us. He does not reduce His interaction with us to our good actions. He sees and loves us unconditionally, hard as that is to accept. We were made good in the beginning; it's who we are. Yes, we fell, but God has dealt with that in Christ. We are now Easter people, called to trust in that work of salvation. God is a God of reality, not unreality. He is with you in all your mess, and He is not surprised by it. This recognition of God's ultimate victory, His love for us, and His presence with us through all things will lead us to greater rest and peace in the world. We need to accept with serenity our true selves as imperfect sons and daughters of God made perfect by the One who is perfect.

Breathe.

You are a beautiful mess.
You are His beloved.

———————— ✠ ————————

You are called to navigate this life with God, His grace moving its way through the chaos of your life.

God works in our human fragility . . .

and it is simply glorious.

Beloved.

ACKNOWLEDGMENTS

I am deeply grateful to my wife, Jenny, for her wisdom and patience with me while I have been writing. Without her support, I simply would not be where I am. I would also like to thank the team of people who have helped me complete this book: my agent, Andrea, from The Bindery, whose belief in me has been steadfast; Danika, my editor; and Jon, my publisher from Tyndale. These wonderful people have guided, encouraged, and challenged me in my writing, all of which I have needed.

Thank you, and may God bless you all.

NOTES

CHAPTER 1: WHO AM I?

1. *Online Etymology Dictionary*, s.v. "understand (*v.*)," accessed September 18, 2023, https://www.etymonline.com/word/understand.

2. C. S. Lewis, *The Problem of Pain* (San Francisco: HarperOne, 2001), 33.

3. Thomas Merton, *New Seeds of Contemplation* (New York: New Directions, 2007), 60.

CHAPTER 3: LISTEN TO THE WHISPERS OF TRUTH

1. Belle Wong, "Top Social Media Statistics and Trends of 2023," Forbes Advisor, May 18, 2023, https://www.forbes.com/advisor/business/social-media-statistics/.

CHAPTER 5: FOLLOW ME

1. Athanasius, *Life of Antony*, in *Early Christian Lives,* trans. Carolinne White (London: Penguin, 1998), 34.

2. Benedicta Ward, trans., *The Sayings of the Desert Fathers: The Alphabetical Collection*, rev. ed. (Trappist, KY: Cistercian Publications, 1984), xiv.

3. *Sayings of the Desert Fathers*, xxi.

CHAPTER 6: BE STILL

1. Benedicta Ward, trans., *Sayings of the Desert Fathers: The Alphabetical Collection*, rev. ed. (Trappist, KY: Cistercian Publications, 1984), 9.

2. Mother Teresa, *In My Own Words*, José Luis González-Balado, comp. (Liguori, MO: Liguori Publications, 1996), 8.

CHAPTER 7: OPEN MY EYES

1. Paul Vasquez (@Yosemitebear62), "Yosemitebear Mountain Double Rainbow 1-8-10," posted on January 8, 2010, YouTube video, 3:29, https://www.youtube.com/watch?v=OQSNhk5ICTI.

CHAPTER 8: WAKE UP TO WONDER

1. Brother Ugolino Boniscambi, *The Little Flowers of Saint Francis*, trans. Jon M. Sweeney (Brewster, MA: Paraclete, 2011).

2. "Taking of the Bread and Wine," *Westcott House Thursday Community Eucharist*, https://www.churchofengland.org/sites/default/files/2019-06/11-westcott-house-creation-eucharist.pdf.

CHAPTER 9: GOD LOVES THE WORLD

1. "The Canticle of the Creatures," in Regis J. Armstrong, J. A. Wayne Hellmann, and William J. Short, eds., *Francis of Assisi: Early Documents* (New York: New City Press, 1999), 1:113–114.

CHAPTER 11: LET GO

1. Brother Ugolino Boniscambi, "St. Francis and Brother Leo Have Trouble Praying Together," in *The Little Flowers of Saint Francis*, trans. Jon M. Sweeney (Brewster, MA: Paraclete, 2011).

CHAPTER 14: THE STATE OF YOUR SOUL

1. John Joseph Myers, "A Theological Reflection on the Human Body," Eternal Word Television Network, 2002, https://www.ewtn.com/catholicism/library/theological-reflection-on-the-human-body-3741.

CHAPTER 15: SPIRITUAL FORMATION

1. R. S. Thomas, as quoted in Martin Laird, *Into the Silent Land: A Guide to the Christian Practice of Contemplation* (New York: Oxford University Press, 2006), 19.

2. Sally Foster-Fulton, *Dancing in the Desert: Prayers and Reflections for Lent* (Glasgow, UK: Wild Goose Publications, 2016), 20.

CHAPTER 17: COME NEAR TO GOD

1. Benedicta Ward, trans., *The Sayings of the Desert Fathers: The Alphabetical Collection*, rev. ed. (Trappist, KY: Cistercian Publications, 1984), 71–72.

2. Mathilde De Robien, "A Technique from the Desert Fathers to Control Our Negative Thoughts," Aleteia, April 14, 2018, https://aleteia.org/2018/04/14/a-technique-from-the-desert-fathers-to-control-our-negative-thoughts/.
3. *Sayings of the Desert Fathers*, 109–110.
4. *Sayings of the Desert Fathers*, 138–139.
5. Richard Rohr, *The Universal Christ: How a Forgotten Reality Can Change Everything We See, Hope For, and Believe* (New York: Convergent Books, 2019), 33.

CHAPTER 19: DISCOVER DEEP REST

1. "On Quiet," Monastery of Christ in the Desert, https://christdesert.org/prayer/desert-fathers-stories/on-quiet/.
2. Augustine, *Confessions*, trans. Henry Chadwick (New York: Oxford University Press, 1998), 3.
3. Benedicta Ward, trans., *The Sayings of the Desert Fathers: The Alphabetical Collection*, rev. ed. (Trappist, KY: Cistercian Publications, 1984), 21–22.
4. William Butler Yeats, "The Balloon of the Mind," https://poets.org/poem/balloon-mind.
5. Charlotte Brontë, *The Professor* (New York: Penguin, 1989), 234.

CHAPTER 20: SURRENDER

1. Constance de la Warr, trans., *The Mirror of Perfection: Being a Record of Saint Francis of Assisi Ascribed to His Companion Brother Leo of Assisi* (London: Burnes and Oates, 1902), 90.

CHAPTER 21: GOD BECAME A BABY

1. Brother Ugolino Boniscambi, "How St. Francis Made Friar Masseo Turn Round and Round Many Times, and Thereafter Gat Him to Siena," in *The Little Flowers of Saint Francis*, trans. Jon M. Sweeney (Brewster, MA: Paraclete, 2011).
2. Thomas of Celano, *The Lives of S. Francis of Assisi*, trans. Alan George Ferrers Howell (London: Methuen and Company, 1908), 92–93.

ABOUT THE AUTHOR

Chris Lee is the vicar of a growing church in London, England, and founder of the Young Franciscans, a new monastic movement for young people. He is an influencer (@revchris7) on Instagram and on YouTube with over 350 million views of the videos that feature him. His sixty-second sermons have brought him national coverage in the United Kingdom. Former *This Morning* presenter Holly Willoughby called him "the internet's favorite vicar." Chris speaks at various conferences and on his podcast, *Come Read with Me*. He is also a contributor to the BBC radio show *Pause for Thought*.